Light the Road of Freedom

WOMEN'S VOICES FROM GAZA

Light the Road of Freedom

SAHBAA AL-BARBARI

Ghada Ageel
& Barbara Bill
Editors

UNIVERSITY
of ALBERTA
PRESS

Published by

University of Alberta Press
1-16 Rutherford Library South
11204 89 Avenue NW
Edmonton, Alberta, Canada T6G 2J4
Amiskwacîwâskahikan | Treaty 6 |
Métis Territory
uap.ualberta.ca

LIBRARY AND ARCHIVES CANADA
CATALOGUING IN PUBLICATION

Title: Light the road of freedom / Sahbaa
    Al-Barbari ; Ghada Ageel and Barbara
    Bill, editors.
Names: Al-Barbari, Sahbaa, author. | Ageel,
    Ghada, 1970- editor. | Bill, Barbara,
    1956- editor.
Description: Series statement: Women's
    voices from Gaza series | Includes
    bibliographical references.
Identifiers: Canadiana (print) 20210189444 |
    Canadiana (ebook) 20210189622 |
    ISBN 9781772125443 (softcover) |
    ISBN 9781772125689 (EPUB) |
    ISBN 9781772125702 (PDF)
Subjects: LCSH: Al-Barbari, Sahbaa. |
    LCSH: Women, Palestinian Arab—
    Gaza Strip—Gaza—Biography. |
    LCSH: Women, Palestinian
    Arab—Gaza Strip—Gaza—Social
    conditions—20th century. |
    LCSH: Women political activists—
    Gaza Strip—Gaza—Biography. |
    LCSH: Gaza Strip—Social conditions—
    20th century. | LCSH: Gaza Strip—
    History—20th century. |
    LCGFT: Autobiographies.
Classification: LCC DS126.6.A45 A3 2021 |
    DDC 956.94/305092—dc23

First edition, first printing, 2021.
First printed and bound in Canada by
Houghton Boston Printers, Saskatoon,
Saskatchewan.
Copyediting and proofreading by
Angela Pietrobon.
Maps by Wendy Johnson.

University of Alberta Press is committed
to protecting our natural environment.
As part of our efforts, this book is printed
on Enviro Paper: it contains 100% post-
consumer recycled fibres and is acid- and
chlorine-free.

University of Alberta Press gratefully
acknowledges the support received for its
publishing program from the Government
of Canada, the Canada Council for the
Arts, and the Government of Alberta
through the Alberta Media Fund.

To those who struggle for justice.

Contents

Preface

Introducing Women's Voices from Gaza

THIS BOOK is the second volume of a series on Women's Voices from Gaza. This series of seven stories recounts life in Palestine, prior to and after its destruction, narrated by women who lived through those experiences. The collected corpus of their accounts offers a detailed and vivid picture of places and people, of both the past and present, of a people. It traces Gaza's history, a rich tapestry woven of many strands.

The oral history accounts recorded in this series complement a body of work asserting the centrality of the narrative of Palestinians in reclaiming and contextualizing Palestinian history. The research, through which these testimonies were located, solicited, documented, and gathered into a whole, aims to re-orient the story of Palestine by restoring it to its original narrator: the Palestinian people. In addition, the focus of this series is on Palestinians who lived in the Gaza Strip, whether prior to, or as a result of, the *Nakba*, the 1948 catastrophe that led to the collective dispossession of the Palestinian people.

While other works, such as that of anthropologist and historian Rosemary Sayigh, have aimed at "narrating displacement"[1] as a defining experience of Palestinian people in modern times, this series describes life both before and after the *Nakba* as it was lived by the narrators: in different parts of Palestine, in Yaffa, Beit Affa, Beit Daras, Beit Hanoun, Khan Younis, Bureij, and Gaza, and in exile. More specifically, it provides a full account of life in different parts of historic Palestine, starting from pre-*Nakba* times, through the destruction of Palestine's villages and towns and the dispossession of their inhabitants in 1948, to the Israeli invasion and occupation during the Swiss crisis in 1956, the war followed by military occupation in 1967, displacement and exile, and two *Intifadas*, to a failed peace process leading to the current impasse. While the series brings to the forefront experiences of normal life before displacement, dispossession, exile, wars, and occupation, the accounts also brilliantly illuminate much of the small, everyday detail of lives in villages and towns. They recount rituals associated with agrarian cycles, wedding rites, rites accompanying birth and death, as well as aspirations, fears, and hopes. Readers are invited to reimagine Palestine and the lives of those sidelined by traditional history.

Unlike some approaches, where essentialized framing of oral histories collected from displaced and refugee women has allowed researchers to "reinterpret" the outcomes of their research, our narrators own and have determined their narratives. Consequently, these are presented in all their complexity, fertility, and normality. Through their deep collective memories, each individual woman transmitted her own narrative/history, embodying a chapter of Palestine's neglected history. Following Edward Said's observation that, "facts get their importance from what is made of them in interpretation...for interpretations depend very much on who the interpreter is, who he or she is addressing, what his or her purpose is, at what historical moment the interpretation takes place,"[2] our effort has been to seek out and foreground the narratives of Palestinian women with minimal interference. This has allowed the women unhindered ownership of their own story, with only minimal intervention or interpretation on our part. Our sole interference in each woman's text was editing and positioning it so as to give it greater fluidity and allow it to read as a cohesive piece.

In contrast to works that have focused on women living in urban areas or on experiences of displacement, this series engages with women from both the urban and rural parts of the Gaza Strip, and with Indigenous women as well as refugees and returnees (women who had been exiled and were able to return to Gaza following the Oslo Accords). Although Gaza is small, it is densely populated, and small geographic variances may have significant impacts on how life is experienced. Life in rural parts of the Strip can be very different from urban life, and Indigenous vs. refugee backgrounds make for distinctly different life stories. Such considerations help move us toward a more fully comprehensive and representative account of life in this part of historic Palestine, both prior to and after 1948.

Unsurprisingly, many of the details of the stories recorded in this series overlap, although the women telling them are unlikely to have met each other. This universality of experience provides a multi-layered map in which human history becomes political history, allowing readers an opportunity to see into the heart of life as it was lived in these spaces from day to day. Individually and as a cumulative corpus, the stories offer a new contribution to the fields of both Palestinian oral history and women's studies.

The life stories collected and presented are those of women from distinct, differing backgrounds: a refugee from

Beit Daras village living in the southern part of the Gaza Strip (Khadija Salama Ammar, Khan Younis refugee camp); a refugee from Beit Affa village living in the central Gaza Strip (Um Jaber Wishah, Bureij refugee camp); a refugee from Yaffa City living in the north of the Strip (Um Said Al-Bitar, Hay Al-Naser in Gaza City); a villager living in the north of the Gaza Strip (Um Baseem Al Kafarneh, the border town of Beit Hanoun); an Indigenous Christian resident of Gaza City (Hekmat Al Taweel); a returnee to the Gaza Strip, originally a resident of Gaza City who was displaced and became a refugee after the 1967 war (Sahbaa Al-Barbari); and an Indigenous resident of the Gaza Strip living in Khan Younis City who subsequently moved to Gaza City (Madeeha Hafez Albatta).

The seven participants were interviewed over two years in the midst of an acutely difficult period: the late 2000s during the second *Intifada*, while freedom of movement within the Gaza Strip was severely restricted. The women interviewed were carefully selected to represent a variety of backgrounds, whether religious or socio-economic, with different personal statuses and very distinct trajectories. Several parameters such as refugee vs. Indigenous background or rural vs. urban experiences determined the editors' selection of interviewees, in an attempt to record Gazan women's knowledge from a broad spectrum of individual standpoints.

We interviewed each woman in her home or on her farm. In most cases, we met with and interviewed them on their own. In some cases, other family members were present. Interviews in the presence of younger people and particularly in the presence of daughters-in-law tended to arouse a great deal of excitement and astonishment, often expressed in a mixture of laughter and tears. These occasions were clearly learning experiences, enabling others as well as the interviewers to join these brave women in exploring and narrating hidden chapters of their lives. Each of our interviewees courageously revealed moments of pain, joy, distress, peace, and uncertainty, along with the abiding hope that they had sustained over decades.

Our interviews with each of the women were audio-taped, producing hundreds of tapes that were then carefully transcribed and translated. One of us is a native speaker of Arabic, which facilitated the translations, and the other is a native speaker of English, which much improved the abbreviated English narratives. In a thorough, nuanced process, we returned to each interviewee with multiple questions and requests for clarification, with the result that the research and editing required a full three years. We checked factual details against known events to ensure the accuracy of each story, which we compiled in a way that would ensure the narrative's continuity, cohesion, and harmony.

The narratives, translated as they were told, remain faithful, honest accounts of these women's lives.

Foreword
An Ode to Sahbaa

GHADA AGEEL, one of the editors of this book, is a Badrasawi. An accomplished academic, a writer, a strong Palestinian voice for justice, and also a good friend. She is all of that, but, above everything, she is a Badrasawi. This means that Ageel's ancestral roots go back to Beit Daras, a small and proud Palestinian village that existed since time immemorial in the southern meadows of Palestine.

Beit Daras only exists in memory now. The village itself— its humble dwellings, its ever-lush citrus orchards, and its historic Great Mosque—were all erased as soon as Zionist militias, which later merged to form the Israeli Defense Forces, took over in May 1948.[1] The Badrasawis bravely and desperately fought for their peaceful village because, for them, Beit Daras represented the entirety of Palestine. It was their extended family, their community—in fact, it was their whole world. There, they learned how to fall in love, how to tend to the land, how to raise children and care for animals, and also how to live and, when necessary, even die together.

Although Beit Daras now exists as a virtual dot on a map of death and destruction, stitched over the course of seventy years of settler colonialism, it is carved indelibly in the minds and hearts of all Badrasawis. Collectively, they carry

Beit Daras with them wherever they go, as will their children and their children's children.

I am a Badrasawi, too. My grandparents built a life there. When the village was set ablaze by advancing Haganah soldiers, something within my grandfather, Mohammed, died forever. He battled depression for the remainder of his life, starting with the *Nakba*—the catastrophic destruction of historic Palestine in 1948. I remember him, often hunched over in his small wooden chair, almost always in complete solitude, rarely moving, except to chase after the patches of little sunlight that trickled through the small courtyard of his humble refugee dwelling, or to pray, whenever the call for prayer summoned him.

My grandmother, Zainab, a woman whose strength was on full display even before the dispossession wrought by the *Nakba*, had to step up. She raised a family under impossible conditions. She worked alongside her husband as a day labourer, breaking rocks in the Gaza Valley. The money they earned by selling their backbreaking daily "harvest" was barely enough to purchase a few items from the makeshift refugee market in Nuseirat, so that they might keep their six children alive. I remember Zainab always moving about, even in old age, caring for everyone, creating a routine within the margins of an unpredictable life. Without her, the family would have broken up. Thanks to Zainab, the family remained intact.

As for my grandfather, I loved him dearly. His humble demeanor and kind words, however little he spoke, reassured me that the world was still a good place, despite our endless exile, even under military occupation. As a child, I assumed that he was a man of few words, only to discover, later, that it was his deep sadness, his irreversible loss, that had taken away his once thunderous voice. He carried the unfulfilled hope of returning to Beit Daras, "when the world wakes up to the injustice carried out by the Zionists." He now lies in an eroding grave within very close proximity, as if embracing the smaller grave, to his ever-faithful wife, Zainab, and surrounded by thousands of refugees who perished while holding on to hope that, someday, they too would all return to Beit Daras, Beit Affa, Hamameh, Isdud, and the hundreds of other villages and towns from which they were so unjustly uprooted.

Collectively, the stories of those who have died, and those who are still living, are the most accurate depiction of the Palestinian story as a whole. Without these stories, the complexity and the inclusion of the Palestinian narrative cannot be fairly or accurately communicated or truly comprehended.

To a great extent, traditional history has failed Palestinians. For one, the historical foundation of the mainstream understanding of the so-called "Arab-Israeli conflict" was laid down by Western historians, who either viewed Palestine from a colonial mindset and/or a Zionist perspective, thus marginalizing the Palestinian as a lesser being, an obstacle in the face of progress and civilization, or altogether contended whether Palestinians even existed as a people in the first place.[2] While historical academic research in many universities is slowly parting ways with such a chauvinistic mindset, the archaic view of Palestine as an arid space that was turned into a paradise, thanks to the ingenuity of Zionist European colonialists, still largely governs Western—though, most notably, American—foreign policy thinking on Palestine and Israel. The utter disregard of Palestinian rights as the foundation of a just peace can be palpably observed, almost daily, in

Western corridors of power. Similarly, there exists a clear pro-Israel bias in US-Western corporate media, where the Palestinian is hardly a victim, but often an aggressor, never a freedom fighter, but always a terrorist.

The second reason why Palestinian stories are rarely considered as a core element in the history of Palestine is related to the elitism of most historical narrations; the nonsensical "Great Man Theory," which, for many years, degraded the significance of seemingly ordinary people in how history is recorded, written, and understood, is one example. While such elitism has been widely rejected and discredited in academic research in many parts of the world, it still reigns supreme when applied to Palestine. In this version of history, Palestinians barely matter as individuals, and are often depicted in a negative light; as factions, they are often derided for their dysfunctional politics and, sadly, as victims who are at times even blamed for their own plight. In this so-called "history," neither of my grandparents' legacies are of any consequence, nor are those of the millions of refugees like them. Their lives, their struggles, and their tragic deaths are meant to be confined to their isolated lives in overcrowded refugee camps or in negligible memories of a bygone era.

Finally, Palestinians have been denied their central place in history because many historians, and, subsequently, many students of history, have been indoctrinated to believe that feelings and emotions have no place in objective, accurate narratives and rigorous academic research; that only geopolitics and geopoliticians matter; that heroes and heroines are politicians and state crafters, and are rarely simple folk, like peasants, workers, teachers, and everyday men and women. Italian intellectual, and, in my view, the world's leading "organic intellectual," Antonio Gramsci wrote about the "intellectual's error"—and, by extension, the "historian's error"—from his prison cell during Italy's Fascist era, nearly a century ago: "The intellectual's error consists in believing that one can know without understanding and even more without feeling and being impassioned." Further, he wrote,

> ...in other words that the intellectual can be an intellectual (and not a pure pedant) if distinct and separate from the nation-people, that is, without feeling the elementary passions of the people, understanding them and therefore explaining and justifying them in the particular historical situation and connecting them dialectically to the laws of history and to a superior conception of the world, scientifically and coherently elaborated—i.e. knowledge.[3]

How can a historian on Palestine, or any other similar history, claim true knowledge if she is "distinct and separate" from the people, neither able to relate to them directly nor, at least, harbour the feeling of their "elementary passions"? This is precisely why I began this text by stating that Ageel is a Badrasawi, because, by being one, she is organically linked to the only authentic "body politic" that matters in the story of all other Badrasawis, themselves a representation of all the refugees—their hopes, their aspirations, but also their persisting tragedy, their fathomable anger, and their legitimate resistance. It is this "positionality," which can be ascribed to the author of this book, that allows Ageel to be the most rational choice as a truly representative historian, genuinely qualified to offer an alternative elucidation on Palestinian history and, by extension, on the Palestinian present and future as well.

It is befitting that Ageel met her co-editor, Barbara Bill, in Gaza. Their relationship and friendship developed there, initially as teacher and student and eventually as scholars sharing the same passion for "authentic Palestinian history"; but they also share cynicism, if not frustration, over the reductionism in the way the world's media has viewed Palestine and totally marginalized the Palestinians themselves, whose stories—rife with *Sumud* (steadfastness), hope, and hardship—represent the only story of Palestine truly worth telling and recording.

Sahbaa's account of her life, presented here by Ageel and Bill, is one such story. Al-Barbari is not only the quintessential Palestinian woman, fighting against immense pressures from without—colonialism and military occupation—as well as from within— Arab betrayal and the stifling patriarchy— but she is also the quintessential Palestinian. In one single story, the reader will locate many of the markers that define Palestinian history as a whole: exile, resistance, imprisonment, defiance, honour, and much more.

Certainly, the story is not that of Al-Barbari alone, for this Palestinian woman's life represents the wider narrative of generations of Palestinian women whose experiences vary in the specifics, but will, most certainly, always converge around numerous meeting points. In the Palestinian narrative, the individual and the collective are rarely separable. This is because rarely in history do entire nations suffer an equal fate within relatively limited scopes of time and space: the *Nakba*, exile, military occupation and its subsequent exiles, routine wars, perpetual sieges, and so on.

History is political. This is why a single event can produce multiple histories. Palestinian history, like the Palestinian people, has also suffered the failures and setbacks of politics.

The 1993 Oslo Accord, in particular, was a critical juncture that shattered the cohesiveness of the Palestinian discourse and weakened and divided the Palestinian people. It reduced the Palestinian experience to clichés centred around futile negotiations and a fraudulent "peace process," while often entirely neglecting the reality on the ground. Under Oslo, the Palestinian people ceased to matter, not only in politics and media reporting but in historical research as well. However, it is not too late to remedy this, through decisive and concerted efforts that overcome the challenge of a political viewpoint on Palestine beholden to self-seeking political aspirations and competing factions. In the absence of a Palestinian leadership populated by the Palestinian people themselves, intellectuals must safeguard and present the Palestinian story to the world with authenticity and balance. The clarity and integrity of the Palestinian story has been damaged and divided by Palestinian Authority tactics, which has long removed the right of return for Palestinian refugees from its political platform.

Perhaps, most importantly, if the story of the Palestinian people is to be told accurately and constructively, the storyteller must be a Palestinian. This is not a veiled ethnocentric sentiment, but, rather, a confirmation that facts change in the process of interpretation, as explained by the late Palestinian professor Edward Said: "Facts get their importance from what is made of them in interpretation... Interpretations depend very much on who the interpreter is, who he or she is addressing, what his or her purpose is and at what historical moment the interpretation takes place."[4]

Intentionally or unwittingly, traditional history has assigned the Palestinian people the role of dislocated, disinherited, and nomadic people without caring about the ethical and political implications of such false representations. Discounting and stereotyping Palestinians in such ways has erroneously presented them as a docile and submissive collective, to be wiped out by those more powerful. Nothing could be further from the truth, and Palestinian resistance is the unremitting example of the strength and resilience of the Palestinian people. Yes, the fight has been an arduous one. Between the rock of Israeli occupation and Hasbara and the hard place of the Palestinian leadership's acquiescence and failure, Palestine, Palestinians, and their story have been trapped and misconstrued.

It is incumbent upon us—not only Palestinians, but those who wish to present a truthful understanding of our historic struggle—to reclaim the Palestinian narrative and dislocate the propaganda-driven Zionist one. The story must now focus wholly on the lives, perspectives, and representations of ordinary people—refugees, the displaced, the poor, the underclass, and working-class Palestinians. It is they who truly epitomize Palestine.

This book honours the life of Sahbaa Al-Barbari, and, by extension, restores some of the dignity to the untold story of all Palestinians.

RAMZY BAROUD

Acknowledgements

THIS BOOK and series would not have been possible
without the support and love of several people who were
extremely generous with their time, comments, directions
and encouragement. For all of them, we are sincerely grateful
and are eternally indebted.

We will begin by expressing our appreciation to the amazing
seven narrators of this series, Sahbaa, Madeeha, Hekmat,
Khadija, Um Bassim, Um Jaber, and Um Said, and their families, for so generously sharing their stories and making us
welcome in their homes.

We are grateful to our friend Shadia Al Sarraj for her
friendship, remarkable support and encouragement.

We would like also to thank Peter Midgley and Mathew
Buntin, the amazing editors at University of Alberta Press,
who helped us throughout the process of writing by answering
queries and providing support. A special thank you to Cathie
Crooks for all her incredible support and to all the talented
team at University of Alberta Press.

Sincere thanks to John Pilger, Wayne Sampey and the
late Inga Clendinnen for their assistance, support and
encouragement.

Several people have generously expended time and effort to read sections of our work and offered valuable advice. Professor Rosemary Sayigh deserves special thanks for her generosity in providing us with useful comments. Sincere thanks go to Rela Mazali for her comments on the work and editing skills. We are also grateful to Terry Rempel and Eóin Murray for reading and commenting on parts of the Introduction. Special thanks and unending gratitude to Andrew Karney for all his support, encouragement and friendship. We also would like to thank Wejdan Hamdan for helping in transcribing the stories. She has dedicated many hours in support of this project that she calls a labour of love and resistance.

Finally, thanks to our late parents, who never gave up hope that these narratives would be published.

Introduction

IN PERFORMING their assigned gender roles as life-givers, xxv
keepers of family tradition, and culture bearers, Palestinian
women have created, practiced, and continue today to practice forms of resistance to generations of oppression that are
largely underreported and unacknowledged. This is the case
in virtually every part of historic Palestine, but it is particularly true of the Gaza Strip. The Gaza Strip, often referred to
simply as "Gaza," is a small, hot button territory on the eastern
shore of the Mediterranean Sea, 40 kilometres long, with a
width that varies from 6 kilometres in the north to some 12
kilometres in the south. Despite its significance as the heart-
land of the Palestinian struggle for freedom and rights, the
history of the place and its people is often deformed by
simplified discourses or reduced to a humanitarian problem
and a contemporary war story. The recurring pain and loss
its people face are offset by life and vibrancy, by playful and
earnest children, by ambitions and dreams.

Around 1.4 million refugees[1] live inside the Gaza Strip
(forming some 18 percent of a worldwide total of 7.9 million
Palestinian refugees[2]). For Palestinians and Palestinian refugees in general, but especially for those living in Gaza, the
central event in the narrative of their lives is the *Nakba*

(the 1948 catastrophe), which led to the dispossession of the Palestinian people, displacing them, appropriating their homes, and assigning them the status of "refugee." In the history of Palestine and Gaza, the catastrophe of collective dispossession is a shared focal point around which they can congregate, remember, organize, and "struggle to reverse this nightmare."[3] Rather than allowing the memory of the *Nakba* to dissipate, time has deepened and extended the communal consciousness of sharing "the great pain of being uprooted, the loss of identity."[4]

In his anguished plea for the departure of "those who pass between fleeting words," the Palestinian national poet Mahmoud Darwish calls for the departed to leave behind "the memories of memory."[5] Darwish's poem is a cry for the value of memory, for the deployment of words, stories, and narratives in the battle for justice. Words and memories, Darwish said, matter. But he also recognized that dispossession is a function of the Palestinian national story. Among the list of items stolen are the blueness of the sea and the sand of memory. These phrases could be references to numerous sites in historic Palestine, but Gaza would have to be among them. There, the blueness of the sea is still available to Palestinians, but the sands of its beaches offer little comfort to those who remain uprooted from the soil of their ancestral homes. (Among them, one of the editors of this work who grew up a short distance from one of Gaza's most famous beaches, Al Mawasi, looking at it from among the dense, grey crowd of houses that make up the Khan Younis refugee camp.)

In Palestinian legal, political, social, and historical discourses, the *Nakba* constitutes the key turning point. The rights to which Palestinians are entitled under international

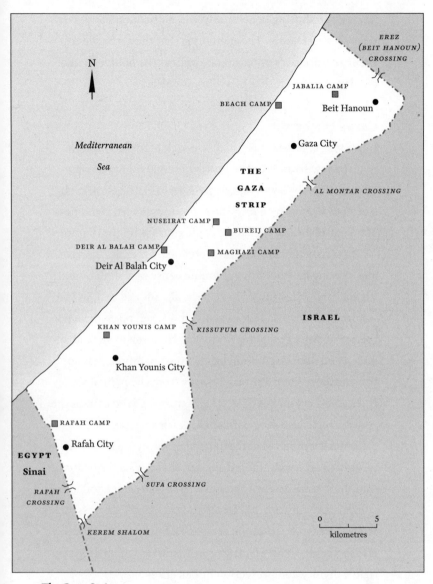

The Gaza Strip.

law are the shifting benchmarks these discourses and narratives seek to restore. The memories that they struggle to keep alive are sites of resistance against the obliteration of history and the erasure of a vibrant culture.

Gaza's History

In putting together this series, we seek to bring attention to just a few strands of the myriad individual narratives comprising the Gazan tapestry. As we explain below, each story has been woven into the series in nuanced awareness

of how it relates to the larger context unfolding at the time.

This larger story is multi-faceted. However, its discrete and varying facets share a common sense of abandonment. Virtually all Palestinians have been abandoned and, in fact, suppressed. That this suppression has taken place through the actions of a group of people who themselves were abandoned and oppressed is one of the most painful ironies of this conflict. When Palestinians cry from the pain of their *Nakba*, this cry comes directly as a mirror of the pain of the Jewish Holocaust—the pain of the Jewish people escaping concentration camps and genocide in Europe. There were cases of people who wanted shelter, security, and freedom. And there were cases of those driven by the Zionist ideology, which, since the days of Herzel and the Basel Congress of 1897, placed a premium on securing a homeland for the Jewish people above all other considerations, including the rights, dignity and protection of Palestinians.

Palestinians have been abandoned by the world, whether by colonial protectorates, like Britain, who signed over "their" land to the Jewish people through the 1917 Balfour Declaration—violating the well-established legal maxim that nobody can give what he does not possess—or by some of

Palestine, 1947: districts and district centres during the British
Mandate period.

today's Arab regimes, mainly the Gulf countries led by Saudi Arabia, who view their common enmity for Iran as justification for steadily siphoning off the rights of Palestinians. The latter creates a sense that the Palestinian cause has lost its status as *cause célèbre* of the region and that the Palestinian people are becoming mere footnotes in regional politics. Perhaps most tragically of all, they have been abandoned by both recent and current Palestinian leadership, who have signed peace deals without addressing the core issues of their struggle: the right of return and the 1948 *Nakba*.

It is no wonder, then, that a second strand of the Palestinian narrative is that of alienation from, and lack of faith in, the political structures that should supposedly achieve legitimacy for the rights that Palestinians yearn for so passionately.

Gaza, from a bird's-eye view, has always been subject to abandonment and suppression. Its location is of strategic significance: a crossroads between Palestine and the lands to the south (Egypt), Israel (today) to the north, and Europe to the west. The future capital of the unborn Palestinian state, occupied East Jerusalem, is just a short hour-and-a-half drive to the east. Under the British Mandate (1922 to 1948), Gaza was one of the six districts of Palestine. When the United Nations voted to partition the country in 1947, Gaza was to be one of the main ports for the future Palestinian state. Successive Israeli governments have consistently deemed the place and its people a problem and perpetual security threat. In idiomatic Hebrew, the expression "go to Gaza" means "go to hell."[6] Even within the Palestinian narrative, Gaza's history has been pushed into the margins.

The UN library contains a vast body of documentation of the processes and consequences of Palestinian dispossession and occupation, whether economic, social, or legal. Alongside the catalogue of resolutions concerning peace, statehood, and rights (UN Resolutions 181, 194, and 242), the UN has also described the Palestinian refugee situation as "by far the most protracted and largest of all refugee problems in the world today."[7]

In 2012, a UN report predicted that Gaza could be rendered completely uninhabitable by 2020.[8] This bizarre prediction is consistent with the notorious Zionist image of Palestine as "a land without a people"[9] This image has now morphed into one in which a piece of that land has become unfit for human habitation, when its inhabitants number far more than they have at any other point in its history. Perhaps this uncomfortable contradiction epitomizes the core of what should be said about the recent history of Gaza in explaining the current Kafkaesque predicament of its civilian population. Undoubtedly, Mahmoud Darwish would have relished its poignant irony.

Gazan life in the early half of the twentieth century was largely agrarian and market based for its eighty thousand inhabitants living in four small towns: Gaza, Deir Al Balah, Khan Younis, and Rafah.[10] Even the most urbane of the Strip's original inhabitants professed a deep connection to the homeland, and the most harried and overextended of Gaza's lawyers and doctors made time to nurture fig trees or raise chickens. However, the situation changed dramatically with the 1948 *Nakba* when over two hundred thousand refugees arrived on the tiny strip of land,[11] after simply travelling down the road without crossing even a single international border, looking for safe haven. Many of them imagined a sojourn in the Strip, probably for a "few days or weeks."[12] Establishment, in 1949, of the United Nations Relief Works

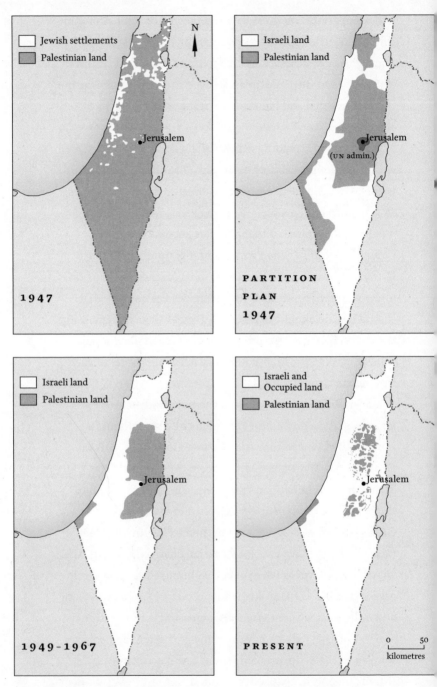

The loss of Palestinian land from 1947 to present.

Agency for Palestinian Refugees (UNRWA) to provide vital services such as education, health care, and social assistance seemed to consolidate the status of these displaced persons, despite their abiding hope for "return." Those who attempted to materialize that hope were forcibly prevented from returning and sometimes killed by Israeli forces. According to Israeli historian Benny Morris, in the period between 1949 and 1956, Israel killed between 2,700 and 5,000 people trying to cross the imaginary line back to their homes.[13] Over time, the tent camps turned into concrete cities, where the politics of resistance incubated that would later flourish.

Egypt controlled the Gaza Strip until 1967. During the Suez Crisis of 1956, Israel occupied the Strip temporarily and committed massacres in Khan Younis and Rafah before Israel's military was forced to withdraw. In Khan Younis alone, Ihsan Al-Agha, a local university teacher, documented the names of hundreds of people killed.[14] This period was signified by the rise of the *Fedayeen* movement—a national movement of Palestinian resistance fighters who attempted to mount attacks against the State of Israel, which had occupied and destroyed their homeland. In order to deter Palestinians, Israel constantly attacked and bombarded Gaza. In August 1953, the Israeli commando force known as Unit 101, under the command of Ariel Sharon, attacked the Bureij refugee camp, east of Gaza City, killing over forty people. Two years later, in 1955, the Khan Younis police station was blown up, leaving seventy-four policemen dead.[15] This period also witnessed tensions between the Egyptians and Palestinians against the backdrop of the Johnson peace proposal in 1955. Endorsed by the UN and the Egyptian government, the proposal sought to re-settle Gazan refugees in the northwest of the Sinai Peninsula. Popular demonstrations protesting the plan were directed against both the UNRWA and the Egyptian administration in Gaza.[16] This wave of focused activism was the context in which the seeds of the Palestine Liberation Organization (PLO) were sown.

The war of 1967, known colloquially as the Six-Day War, left the Gaza Strip and the West Bank occupied by Israel, as well as the Syrian Golan Heights and the Egyptian Sinai Peninsula. Soon after the war, Israel enacted the annexation of East Jerusalem. These developments generated a new set of legal and political structures that extend to the present day. In East Jerusalem, Israeli law applies to all citizens (whether Palestinian or Jewish). However, the Palestinian residents of East Jerusalem are required to hold special ID documents and they are not entitled to Israeli citizenship (unlike the Palestinian Arab citizens of other areas inside Israel, such as Nazareth). In the West Bank and Gaza Strip, the "occupied territories," Israeli military law was applied. When Jewish settlements were introduced (that is, colonial townships for Jewish people planted on occupied Palestinian land), a new legal strand emerged and standard Israeli law was selectively and exclusively applied to the Jewish residents of the West Bank and the Gaza Strip. Such were the emerging features of a regime that has gained increasingly unfavourable comparisons to apartheid rule in South Africa. In Israel and the territories under its control, legal restrictions on people are conditional upon identities and the respective status of these identities within heavily stratified and discriminatory laws. The regime, in other words, implements a "legally sanctioned separation based on discrimination."[17]

The so-called "Six-Day War" of 1967 resulted in the expulsion of another 300,000 Palestinians from their homes, including 130,000 who were displaced for a second time after their initial displacement in 1948.[18] The defeat followed by the military occupation shattered Palestinians' hopes for return, but energized the national movements led by the *Fedayeen*. To pacify resistance in the Strip, then Israeli Defence Minister Sharon initiated a policy of home demolitions that continues to this day. As people in Gaza were subjected to intensified restrictions on freedom of movement and to increasingly squalid economic conditions, it was no accident that the 1987 *Intifada* was first triggered in Gaza, specifically in the Jabalya refugee camp, and rapidly spread across the remainder of the Strip before it was joined by the West Bank. The uprising was a mass popular movement that held up for six years. It manifested in protests and strikes, in civil disobedience, and in boycotts. Unable to supress the masses, Israel shut down Gaza's universities for six years, denying tens of thousands of students the opportunity to study, including one of the editors of this series. It imposed curfews locking the entire Palestinian population of Gaza inside their homes every night for about six years.[19] An order ascribed to Israel's then Defence Minister, Yitzhak Rabin, directed the Israeli army to break the bones of Palestinian protesters.[20] The images of unarmed Palestinian youths throwing rocks at fully armed Israeli troops captured attention in international media and contributed to a narrative of the Palestinian David fighting Israel's Goliath.

Amidst the heat of the *Intifada*, a peace process was launched in Madrid under the auspices of the Americans and the Soviets in 1991. The process eventually culminated with the Oslo Accords, signed by Israel and the PLO on the White House lawn in September 1993. In keeping with the terms of the Accords, the Palestinian Authority (PA), an interim self-governing body, was constituted. The PA, led by the late Yasser Arafat, along with the PLO leadership, were allowed to return to Gaza and establish a headquarters. Oslo was the pinnacle of Palestinian hopes for statehood and self-determination. Widespread discussions stated that Gaza would become the "Singapore of the Middle East."[21] These hopes evaporated, however, when the Accords panned out as the "biggest hoax of the century."[22] They neglected to deal with the core issues of both the conflict and the Palestinian cause: with the Palestinian refugees, with the right of their return, and with the 1948 *Nakba*.[23] Reflecting his deep frustration at the aftermath of the Oslo Accords, Palestinian historian Salman Abu Sitta, himself a refugee expelled to Gaza along with his family, wrote to PLO leader Yasser Arafat, asking him why the Accords and his ensuing speech at the UN had omitted "Palestine," "Palestinians," and demands for inalienable rights:

> *I wished to hear you, Mr. President, say in your speech: I stand before you today to remind you that forty-six years ago 85 percent of my people were uprooted by the force of arms and the horror of massacres, from their ancestral homes. My people were dispersed to the four corners of the earth. Yet we did not forget our homeland for one minute... Let us learn the lesson of history: Injustice will not last. Justice must be done.*[24]

"Oslo," as the Accords are commonly called, entrenched the segregation of Palestinian communities. In 1994, a fence was erected around Gaza; a permit system was applied to anyone who needed to leave the Strip. This had a drastic impact on the population's ability to conduct anything approximating a "normal" life, while severely weakening the Strip's economy.

The failure of Oslo to recognize the core issues at stake for the Palestinian people was followed by the breakdown of negotiations between the PA and Israel in late 2000. This stalemate provided fertile ground for the eruption of the second *Intifada*. Israel's violence in suppressing this uprising unleashed the full might of the world's fifth largest army against a defenceless civilian population. Daily bombings by F-16 fighter jets became the soundtrack of daily life in Gaza, while Palestinians mounted armed attacks against Israeli military posts inside the Strip and against the army and sometimes civilians in Israeli towns and cities.

In 2001, Sharon declared war on the PA's leadership, security officials, and infrastructure. Israeli bulldozers destroyed the runway of Gaza International Airport, attacked the symbols of Arafat's authority, and bombarded and destroyed Arafat helicopters. These attacks left much of Gaza's internationally funded infrastructure in ruins.[25] Even worse, however, as a form of collective punishment of Gazans, Israel imposed a policy of internal "closure," preventing movement within the tiny Strip. It divided the Gaza Strip into three parts. The principal closure points were on the coastal road to the west of the Netzarim colony (formerly located between Gaza City and the Nuseirat camp) and at the Abu Holi Checkpoint (named after the farmer whose land was confiscated to build the checkpoint), located at the centre of the Strip. Each time the Israeli army shut down these points, Gaza was split apart, paralyzing all movement of people and goods.[26] For five consecutive years, for Gazan doctors, nurses, patients, students, teachers, farmers, labourers, and mothers, a trip from north to south—ordinarily a ninety-minute round trip—could turn into a week-long ordeal, and dependence on the kindness of one's extended family for accommodations and food until the checkpoints were re-opened.[27]

In 2004, Dov Weisglass, adviser to Prime Minister Sharon, declared his strategy of rendering the peace *process* moribund and his intention to sink it, along with Palestinians' national dreams, in "formaldehyde."[28]

Israeli political activity has always been rooted in unilateralism. The false narrative of a "land without people" permitted the "people without a land"—now instated in what was formerly Palestine—to conduct themselves in absolute disregard of the existence of another people. The latter, like so many rocks and boulders, were simply to be bulldozed flat as the new state was being constructed. Israel's unilateral disengagement from Gaza in 2005, vacating about eight thousand settlers, whose houses and farms covered forty percent of the area of the Strip, was an act of political sleight of hand that allowed Israel to declare itself free of political and moral responsibility for the Gaza Strip, while also declaring it an "enemy entity"[29] in 2007. It could accordingly be enveloped in a siege designed to generate medieval living conditions.[30]

The 2006 free and fair elections that brought the Islamic resistance movement, Hamas, into power were the fruit created by Israel's departure, viewed by many Palestinians as a victory of the resistance, led by Hamas, to Israel's brutal policies of oppression, as well as to the inherent weakness at the heart of the Palestinian Authority. The latter, which is supposedly authorized to govern, is constrained by severe limitations that effectively disable the centrifugal forces allowing the governance of states. The US and the EU were the parties at whose demand the fledgling Palestinian Authority conducted elections, and these were declared fair and free by all international monitors. And yet, these same parties proceeded to boycott the results (which they found unsatisfactory) and to cut foreign aid to the PA. For the most part, these cuts and the shortages they incurred were imposed upon Gaza (and to a lesser degree, the West Bank).

Declaring Gaza an "enemy entity" allowed Israel to conduct three major offensives against the Strip, in 2008, 2012, and 2014. The 2014 offensive, which lasted 51 days, destroyed much of what had previously functioned as Gaza's infrastructure and institutions, including the complete or partial destruction of at least 100,000 homes, 62 hospitals, 278 mosques, and 220 schools.[31] It also left 2,300 people dead, the majority of these being civilians, and tens of thousands wounded.[32]

Four generations of refugees now live in the Gaza Strip, scattered among eight refugee camps. As of 2021, Gaza is still under siege. Access to the outside world is controlled by Israel, or by Egypt, acting as Israel's sub-contractor. No one can enter or leave the Strip without permits from one of these two powers. According to Oxfam, in 2019, one million Palestinians in Gaza lacked sufficient food for their families. Sixty percent of these Gazans were subsisting on less than $2 a day. Unemployment, measured at 62 percent in 2019, is among the highest in the world.[33] Economist Sara Roy has characterized the pattern as one of structural de-development,[34] and Israeli historian Avi Shlaim describes it as "a uniquely cruel case of intentional de-development" and a "classic case of colonial exploitation in the post-colonial era."[35] Although the World Bank has said that Gaza's economy is in "free fall,"[36] the Strip has in fact maintained a perverse stasis: formaldehyde, after all, is used to preserve corpses.

Israeli sociologist Eva Illouz recently compared the present circumstances of the Palestinian people to conditions of slavery. These conditions, she said, present one of the great moral questions of our time and are similar, in certain respects, to the slavery that embroiled the US in civil war in the nineteenth century.[37]

The strands of oppression and violence running through the Palestinian tapestry are interwoven with strands of endurance, ability to overcome, and *Sumud*—steadfastness—in the face of injustice. Palestinians still firmly believe in return and in the possibility of justice, even if these ideals have become embattled and tattered. Gaza's high level of concentration on the importance of these narratives belies its tiny size, at just 1.3 percent of historic Palestine. Protesting the circumstances of all Palestinians, the near suffocation of the Gaza Strip, and the international disinterest in both, Gazan civil society launched the Great March of Return in 2018. Weekly protests were initiated along the border fence with Israel every Friday, calling on both Israel and the world to recognize the inalienable right of Palestinians to return to the homes and lands from which they were forcibly removed seven decades ago. The protesters also insist upon a plethora of other basic rights denied to Palestinian people in the "ongoing *Nakba*" of their lives.[38] The World Health Organization reported over 300 Gazans were shot and killed by the Israeli army in the course of these rallies, as of December 2019, with 35,000 more injured.[39] On May 14, 2019 alone, Israeli military snipers killed 60 unarmed demonstrators and wounded 2,700.[40]

The weekly marches are an ongoing journey fulfilling the prophesy of Mahmoud Darwish that "a stone from our land builds the ceiling of our sky."[41] Every independent state formed after "the dismantling of the classical empires in the post-World War Two years" has recognized an urgent need "to narrate its own history, as much as possible free of the biases and misrepresentations of that history," as written by colonial historians.[42] In an analogy to the poetry that represents a highly important oral tradition in the Arab world, we see this book as an effort to capture the poetry of life and the history of a people, expressed by those who live it on a daily basis.

Filling in a Tapestry of Resistance Through Memory Work

The history of Gaza is far richer and deeper than the standard narratives of helplessness, humanitarian disaster, or war story would have us believe. Moreover, as is the case with other post-colonial regions and their histories, Gazan history differs greatly from official accounts and Eurocentric renderings based (largely) on oversimplifications.[43] This series is, accordingly, an attempt to replace detached— and sometimes questionable—statistics and chronologies of erupting conflict with some of the concrete details of actual survival and resistance, complex human emotions, and specific difficult choices. The stories recounted reflect crucial facts and important events through the evidence of lived experience. They contextualize selective reports and statistics, correcting omissions, misrepresentations, and misinterpretations.

This series is an attempt to reimagine the history of Gaza from the viewpoint of its people. A true understanding of Gaza entails a reading of the human history beyond and behind chronologies, a reading that follows some of the coloured threads that make its tapestry so vibrant. The seven women whose stories we relate communicate the history they lived, through reflecting on events they experienced in their own voices and vocabularies. They shared feelings and named processes as they understood them, enabling others to grasp and realize the sheer dimensions of the injustice to which they were subjected and which they amazingly withstood.

Israeli New Historian Ilan Pappe has used the term "memoricide" to denote the attempted annihilation of memory, particularly that of the Palestinian *Nakba*. A systematic "erasure of the history of one people in order to write that of another people's over it" has constituted the continuous imposition of a Zionist layer and of nationalized Israeli patterns over everything Palestinian.[44] This has included the erasure of all traces of the Palestinian people— of the recultivation and renaming of Palestinian sites and villages. These practices were recounted victoriously by Moshe Dayan in 1969:

> *We came to this country which was already populated by Arabs and we are establishing a Hebrew, that is, a Jewish state here. Jewish villages were built in the places of Arab villages and I do not know even the names of these Arab villages, and I do not blame you, because the geography books no longer exist, the Arab villages are not there either. Nahalal arose in the place of Mahlul, Kibbutz Gvat in the place of Jibta; Kibbutz Sarid in the place of Huneidi and Kfar Yehushua in the place of Tal al Shuman. There is not a single place built in this country that did not have a former Arab population.*[45]

In the context of daily hardship, then, memory is crucial. It is a deeply significant site for resisting policies of elimination and erasure. Often, such resistance work takes place within families, and, in particular, through women. Stories of lost homes are handed down from generation to generation and repeated time and again, preserving the names of lost villages and towns, detailing former landholdings, passing on deeds, and recounting traditions and tales about "the ancestors, everyday life, the harvests, and even quarrels."[46] When asked where they are from, most of the children of Palestinian refugee families will state the name of a village lost generations ago.

In recognizing women's diverse experiences as a key to decoding history, we share accounts of women of the generation that experienced the 1948 *Nakba*, told with the backdrop of the master narratives of Gaza, offering new insights into the story of Palestine. The respective narrators enable readers to gain a fuller understanding of the scale of tragedy experienced by each of these women and of its socio-economic and political impacts.

The series draws on the concept of "History from Below" proposed by the French historian Georges Lefebvre, who emphasized that history is shaped by ordinary people over extended periods of time.[47] It also draws on the feminist concept of "Herstory," where feminist historians and activists reclaim and retell the suppressed accounts of historical periods as women, particularly marginalized women, experienced them. It is in these traditions that we present the oral histories of Palestinian women from the Gaza Strip. The school of oral history, initiated with tape recorders in the 1940s, achieved increased recognition during the 1960s, and is now considered a major component of historical research that enlists the assistance of twenty-first-century digital technologies.[48] In defending the method of recording oral history, Paul Thompson argued, in *The Voice of the Past: Oral History*, that it transmutes the content of history "by shifting the focus and opening new areas of inquiry, by challenging some of the assumptions and accepting judgment of historians, by bringing recognition to substantial groups of people who had been ignored."[49] The historically "silent" or, more accurately, "silenced" social groups cited by Thompson include Indigenous people, refugees, migrants, colonized peoples, those of subaltern categories, and minorities. Such groups have employed the methodology of oral history to represent the totality of truth and to counteract dominant discourses that suppress their versions of history. Moreover, oral history has been recognized by these groups as a method of realizing their right to own and sound a voice, to write their own history and share their collective experiences, and to resist the dominant colonial rhetoric that omits or obliterates these experiences. In this context, Alistair Thomson argued that "for many oral historians, recording experiences which have been ignored in history and involving people in exploring and making their own histories, continue to be primary justifications for the use of oral history."[50] Oral history, as a method that both enhances and disrupts formal history, has not yet taken root extensively in the Arab world. Among a few rare exceptions, according to anthropologist and historian Rosemary Sayigh, are the Palestinians "who have used oral and visual documents to record experiences of colonialist dispossession and violence that challenge dominant Zionist and Western versions of their history."[51] In gradually moving "from the margins to the center," this practice has come to constitute the core of Palestinian

historiography in the past twenty years,[52] and is deployed
abundantly, both formally and informally, in collecting
and reviving knowledge that was formerly unrecorded.
In response to Edward Said's call for the "permission to
narrate,"[53] oral history has paved the way for the continued
production of archival collections, resisting the ongoing
erasure of Palestinian spaces, existence, history, and identity. Sherna Gluck notes that this method not only recovers
and preserves the past through the collection of accounts,
for example, of the *Nakba*, but also establishes the legitimacy
of claim and of the right of return.[54] For Palestinians such
as Malaka Shwaikh, a Gaza-born scholar, oral history and
memory of the past act "as a force in maintaining and repro-
ducing their rights as the sole owners of Palestine" and as
"fuel for their survival."[55]

Over the past two decades, numerous laypeople, non-
governmental organizations, and solidarity workers have
joined the intellectual mission of rescuing a history that
aims, according to Said, to advance human freedom, rights,
and knowledge.[56] That mission has gathered momentum
and gained significance in historic Palestine in a context of
neglect on the part of the Palestinian national leadership,
which has failed to organize and ensure continuous records
or documentation of popular Palestinian experience and
of the ongoing dangers posed by the Israeli occupation.[57]
The specifics of this violence as a current historical process
were highlighted in a book by Nahla Abdo and Nur Masalha
titled *An Oral History of the Palestinian Nakba* (2018). The
book includes a detailed discussion of the potential of oral
history for historicizing marginal experience. It also notes
that Palestinian history has not been adequately recorded as
the experience of both a community and of individuals and

emphasizes the vital role that oral history plays in assembling the Palestinian narrative.

The role of Palestine during World War II features prominently in standard historiographies, but little has been written about its Indigenous population, the conditions of their existence prior to 1948, or their collective life and history before exile. Summing up this gaping void, Said wrote: "Unlike other people who suffered from a colonial experience, the Palestinians...have been excluded; denied the right to have a history of their own...When you continually hear people say: 'Well, who are you anyway?' you have to keep asserting the fact that you do have a history, however uninteresting it may appear to the very sophisticated world."[58]

Scholarly Work on Palestine's History

Many historians and researchers have drawn on both oral and visual history to counter the multi-form suppression and abandonment—ranging from disinterest to fundamental denial—of Palestinian history recounted from Palestinian standpoints. A variety of strategies have been adopted in carrying out such work, and among these efforts are Ibrahim Abu Jaber et al.'s *Jurh Al-Nakba* (The Wound of Nakba) (2003) and Walid Khalidi's *Before Their Diaspora: A Photographic History of the Palestinians, 1876-1948* (1984). Others have presented individualized narratives, for example, in Salman Abu Sitta's *Mapping My Return: A Palestinian Memoir* (2016), Alex Awad's *Palestinian Memories: The Story of a Palestinian Mother and Her People* (2008), and Leila El-Haddad's *Gaza Mom: Palestine, Politics, Parenting, and Everything In Between* (2010). Scholars such as Ramzy Baroud, in *Searching Jenin: Eyewitness Accounts of the Israeli Invasion 2002* (2003), have

used oral testimonies in more comprehensive works to gain
a fuller understanding of specific events (in this case, Israel's
siege on Jenin in 2002), while linking the event in question
to collective Palestinian history. Others have recounted the
singular history of specific political factions, for instance,
Khaled Hroub in *Hamas: Political Thought and Practice*
(2000) and Bassam Abu Sharif in *Arafat and the Dream of
Palestine: An Insider's Account* (2009). Several online projects
and websites, such as *Palestine Remembered*, have also initiated and continue to maintain an ongoing collection and
dissemination of Palestinian oral histories.[59]

Nakba: Palestine, 1948, and the Claims of Memory (2007),
edited by Ahmad H. Sa'di and Lila Abu-Lughod, is one of the
more prominent attempts to incorporate oral history as an
essential means of delivering history, justice, and legitimacy
for the Palestinian cause, while also linking current events to
the recent past. Departing from the *Nakba* as a central event
that defines and unites Palestinians, their volume undertakes
the injection of collective memory into the overall framework of Palestinian history. Making memory public, Sa'di
and Abu-Lughod write, "affirms identity, tames traumas and
asserts Palestinian political and moral claims to justice, redress
and the right of return."[60] It also challenges the Zionist myth
that Palestinians have no roots in the land.

Some authors have taken up Said's idea of the intellectual's
mission being to advance human freedom and knowledge.[61]
This idea is based on Said's definition of the intellectual as
being both detached and involved—outside of society and its
institutions, and simultaneously a member of society who is
constantly agitating against the status quo. Ramzy Baroud's
book *My Father Was a Freedom Fighter: Gaza's Untold Story*
(2010), the Indigenous section in Ghada Ageel's edited

volume *Apartheid in Palestine: Hard Laws and Harder Experiences* (2016), which includes chapters by Reem Skeik, Samar El Bekai, and Ramzy Baroud, and Palestinian poet Mourid Barghouti's *I Was Born There, I Was Born Here* (2012) are all manifestations of a concept in which the outsider is also the insider, the researcher, and the narrator. The authors of these narratives either spent a large part of their lives under Israel's occupation or returned from exile and experienced the suffering of both the individual and the group. These experiences generated their common aspiration to become intellectuals who would repeatedly disturb and problematize the status quo. In documenting their personal stories and describing everyday life in the West Bank and Gaza, these insider-outsider-researcher-narrators have attempted to link present and past.

Within the broader context of abandoned and suppressed narratives, accounts of women's experiences, elided almost completely from hegemonic histories, open sorely neglected but significant avenues into an understanding of how the past and the present are constituted, reconstituted, and conceived. Women's accounts are particularly vital for comprehending the past and present in Palestine, as they are framed and determined by the ethnic cleansing of 1948. While women's stories are largely marginalized, their experiences form a cornerstone of the structure of human impacts generated by successive military campaigns against Palestinians and by generations of Palestinian resistance, both military and non-violent. Foregrounding women's narratives counteracts a history in which selectiveness reinforces and supports systems of oppression and displacement through the erasure of authentic voices and the prioritization of male-dominant narratives.

The tragedy of 1948 and its aftermath in Palestine have been endured by the whole of society and particularly by women, who have borne the remnants with which to reconstruct lost homes both on their backs and in their hearts. As they have put up and organized tents to house their families, they have cared for and raised children, and queued for hours to receive United Nations rations and handouts of clothes, blankets, and kitchen utensils. They have struggled to keep smiles on their own faces and those of their families in the face of humiliation and bitter pain, in the day-to-day practice of what Palestinians call *Sumud*. Uncovering the details of their life journeys under such exceptional circumstances reveals a version of Palestinian history that is not only far more complete, but that also acknowledges the central role that women have played in making this history. Sayigh has argued that

> *women have been a basic element in the Palestinian capacity to survive poverty, oppression, exile. They have been models of courage, tenacity, resourcefulness and humour. Though all were victims of expulsion and of gender subalternity, I would never think of them primarily in these terms, but rather as people who knew/know how to live against poverty and oppression. Palestinian women have the inner resources to make a good life for their children. They pack, and move, and set up again in a new place, among new people.*[62]

Research on the role of gender in preserving the memory of the *Nakba* has been carried out by several scholars who have attempted to detail and highlight this crucial agency. In their contribution to *Nakba*, edited by Sa'di and Abu

Lughod, Isabelle Humphries and Laleh Khalili used oral history to "examine both how the Nakba is remembered by women, and what women remember about it."[63] It was also crucial to them to investigate how women's memories "were imbricated by both the nationalist discourse and the same patriarchal values and practices that also shape men's lives and their memories."[64] Their chapter confronts the manifold predominant narrative and the resulting lack of confidence that has suppressed women's voices and constrained their role as a conduit of memory.[65] Palestinian women's lack of self-confidence vis-a-vis, and exacerbated by, the male-dominant narrative is clearly reflected, for instance, in Sayigh's quotation from one narrator: "I can't say I know all this history; others know it better." While this narrator is an "eloquent history teller" who is familiar with the events she witnessed, she still designates the task for telling history to those "who would know better."[66]

Fatma Kassem's book, *Palestinian Women: Narrative Histories and Gender Memory* (2011), focuses on Palestinian women living in Israel. Kassem collected the oral testimonies of urban Palestinian women, a group whose life stories of displacement are rarely noted, even though they form essential parts of the larger Palestinian national narrative. Kassem, who was born in today's Israel years after the *Nakba*, positions herself as both an insider—a narrator of her own story—and an outsider—a researcher—in the volume that aims to reveal "the complex intersections of gender, history, memory, nationalism and citizenship in a situation of ongoing colonization and violent conflict between Palestinians and the Zionist State of Israel."[67] Like Baroud, Ageel, and Barghouti, this positionality allowed her a great deal of freedom in crossing boundaries as an unconstrained outsider while interacting intensively as a trusted insider with the other narrators.

The work of Sayigh exhibits a similar type of direct inter-action with the narratives of Palestinian women. She has authored several books examining the oral history of the Palestinians, notably, *The Palestinians: From Peasants to Revolutionaries.*[68] In her work, *Voices: Palestinian Women Narrate Displacement*, an online book, Sayigh narrates the stories of seventy Palestinian women from various locations in the West Bank, the Gaza Strip, and Jerusalem.[69] The inter-viewees spoke about their lives following the displacement of Palestinians after the *Nakba*. Like most of her influential work, Sayigh's interviews—conducted between 1998 and 2000, just prior to the initiation of this project—investigate displacement and its effects on Palestinian women, and the impact of the *Nakba* on the identity of women and their sense of self. Also considered in her book is the linkage between collective displacement and the critical role played by women in the Palestinian narrative. Sayigh's body of work has not only advanced the destabilization of dominant narratives, making space for a more egalitarian narration of history, it also accurately situates Palestinian women at the centre of Palestinian history, offering a fuller, more representative understanding of Palestinian history altogether.

The *Women's Voices from Gaza* series is a continuation of the oral history work carried out by many intellectuals and individuals who aimed to assign Indigenous Palestinians a greater role in explaining the dynamics of their own history and to re-orient the story of Palestine by restoring it to its original narrator: the Palestinians. It is a complement to a corpus of work that preceded this series and that asserts the centrality of the narrative of Palestinians, especially women, in reclaiming and contextualizing their history.

Light the Road of Freedom

Light the Road of Freedom is the second in this series of Women's Voices from Gaza, seven stories recounting life in Palestine prior to and after the 1948 *Nakba*. These accounts offer a vivid and rich picture of places, and of the past and present, and a detailed portrait of a people.

Light the Road of Freedom is the story of a dignified, strong, and outspoken Indigenous Palestinian woman. Her name is Sahbaa Al-Barbari. Sahbaa was born and raised in Gaza, a principal city tucked in the heart of the Strip on the shore of the Mediterranean. After finishing high school, Sahbaa attended Cairo University and earned her Bachelor of Arts in philosophy and psychology. She returned to Gaza in 1957 and commenced her career as a schoolteacher. Since a very young age, she has been active in her community, mobilizing, leading initiatives, and advocating for Palestinian rights. Due to this activism, Sahbaa spent a year behind bars in an Egyptian jail back in 1958, when Gaza was still under the Egyptian administration.

Upon her release, and as punishment for her political activism, she was demoted from her job as a teacher and was obliged to accept an administrative secretarial role in the education department. In 1964, she got married to one of Palestine's most influential and renowned poets, Mu'in Bseiso. Her companionship with Mu'in would take her across several countries in the Arab world as well as European states.

When Israel occupied the Gaza Strip in 1967, Sahbaa and Mu'in became refugees, stripped of their residency rights, and were forced to live in exile for the next three decades. Israel denied them, together with tens of thousands of Palestinians who happened to be outside at the time of the war, their identity cards and hence the right to return to their homes in Gaza. As she hopped from one country to another, Sahbaa would live with uncertainty, experiencing the bitter taste of being uprooted from her land and ultimately becoming stateless. As she moved from place to place, she always held tight to her dream and hope of one day returning to Gaza.

Sahbaa lived in Beirut for eleven years, and spent over a year in Damascus, eight months in Libya, three years in Egypt, and fourteen years in Tunis. Each of these stages of Sahbaa's life speaks volumes about the struggle experienced by millions of Palestinians living in exile, separated from their loved ones and their homeland. Lebanon is only one example. While there, Sahbaa witnessed and lived the horror of the Israeli invasion of 1982. Refusing to leave Mu'in alone during the war and unable to provide protection to her own children or medical care for her mother-in-law, Sahbaa was obliged to make hard decisions. In their search for safety, a friend of Sahbaa's family, a Lebanese journalist, smuggled Sahbaa's children and their ailing grandmother to Damascus by car. When the PLO leadership was evacuated from Lebanon, Sahbaa and Mu'in were among the first group to leave Beirut for Greece. Upon their arrival in Greece, Mu'in continued on his way to London. Sahbaa had to open her eyes to the bitter taste of separation and segregation, a permanent feature of Palestinian life. She was on her own, with her son in one place and her daughters in another, while Mu'in travelled to a different destination, leaving her to decide where to go next.

In her narrative, Sahbaa approximates the collective story of Palestinians living in exile, speaking of the constant sense of uncertainty, fear, and displacement. She also communicates the troubles Palestinians face in airports and at borders due to their status as stateless people. Although Sahbaa was lucky to get papers that allowed her to travel, the cry for denied rights is clearly heard in her narrative when she says, "I am a Palestinian from Gaza who was given an Egyptian travel document to allow me to travel, and then a Jordanian passport to ease my movement. How can it be easy to change from one nationality to another when in the end it is not my own?"

Her story also provides a small window where readers can get a glimpse into life inside Gaza, shedding light on its lively and spirited people, who she suggests embody the phoenix rising from the ashes.

Before telling the story of being forced into exile in 1967, Sahbaa clearly expresses this spirit when she talks about Gaza's grand resistance but also of a living and thriving society, unfolding tales of many of Gaza's intellectuals and civil society leaders, and the remarkable initiatives that occurred during the 1930s to the 1960s. She demonstrates the spirit of Gaza's people, with their high levels of education, fierce aspirations for freedom, and defiance of oppression, and their role as leaders in the struggle against occupation. All of this is a sliver of history more often hidden than exposed.

Among those community leaders portrayed in the narrative is her husband Mu'in, whom Dr. Ramzy Baroud eloquently compared to Gaza itself when he wrote, "The spirit of Gaza is the spirit of Mu'in Bseiso: beautiful, poetic, tortured, strong, undying, and loving and although confined by ever-shrinking spaces, always resisting."[70] These words are the exact words that also describe Sahbaa's spirit and personality.

One of the most shattering moments in her life was the loss of Mu'in. He died behind the walls of a London hotel in 1984. Israel denied his family the permission to have his remains buried in Gaza. So, he was buried in Cairo.

After dreaming of return for about thirty years, Sahbaa returned to Gaza in 1996. She hoped that her return would coincide with an end to the decades of Palestinian suffering. Sadly, this did not happen. Gaza continues to suffer oppression in the form of repeated wars and a suffocating, illegal, immoral, and inhumane blockade. As a result, Sahbaa is again back in exile.

Light
the Road
of Freedom

1 / Growing Up in Gaza

*I always believe that working together in groups or teams
increases one's abilities, making the individual forget the
self, while being part of a collective. You learn through
these interactions, how to agree and disagree, to speak and
to listen, and to respect the opinions and views of others.
By doing so, you also learn to care by being empathetic
to the situation and sympathetic to the problems and
suffering. This is why I always encouraged my students to
be involved in activities, groups, and initiatives, whether
social or political, because through these activities we can
continue to learn and grow.*

I AM AN INDIGENOUS RESIDENT of the Gaza Strip.
I was born in Gaza City in 1932 and was one of eight, with
an older brother, two older sisters, a younger brother, and
two younger sisters. An older sister had died of diphtheria
at the end of the 1920s. Our origins are in Gaza: my mother's
family name is Halawa and my father's family name is
Al-Barbari. Our family cared a lot about education. Although
my mother was illiterate, she insisted that we all receive a
good education and encouraged us to finish university. While
studying at university, I taught her to write the letters of her

name and her signature. One of my sisters is a doctor who married and works in Syria, and my other three sisters, who are teachers or trained as teachers, live in Egypt. My oldest brother studied political and economic science at Cairo University and the other is an electrical engineer. Both of them worked in Libya and then went to Iraq, but they had to leave, as many other Palestinians did, because of some political problems, and now they are in Cairo.

My grandfather owned the Al-Barbari sesame press in Al Daraj, a suburb in the heart of the Old City of Gaza, where the Jabalya taxi station is now, that produced sesame oil and *tahenah* (sesame paste). My father brought sesame in very big sacks on the backs of camels and horses from all the villages in Palestine that produced it, and sometimes from villages in Egypt. There was even a village called *Simsim* (sesame) in Palestine, which I think was famous for sesame. After the sesame was pressed, it was stored in large metal tanks, and the residue was mixed with straw, pressed into cubes, and sold to villagers as food for their animals. There was another sesame press in Gaza called Al Hindi, also in Al Daraj.

My grandfather had a big two-storey house with three bedrooms in Al Daraj, on what became Al Wehda Street in 1967. But before then, the streets were very narrow and crowded with many houses.[1] These houses were very old, with high ceilings and very thick walls, and with water cisterns in the yards. The high ceilings in the house were very practical because they kept the rooms cool and kept out the heat. The same style of architecture is still found in Morocco and Tunis: very thick walls with windows at an angle at the top to let in the breeze. My grandfather's house was open, not closed like they are today, and full of arches and domes. There were murals on the ceilings, and from the centre of them hung candles and *fawanees* (lamps). The walls had deep recesses to store clothing, bedding, and mattresses. My aunt was very clever and made covers for these recesses. She ironed them very neatly, and folded them in a unique way (each garment had a different way that you could fold it to retain its shape). There was no electricity, so the clothes were pressed with a very heavy iron that would be placed on charcoal to heat.

My uncle used to read and work on the second storey, which was reached by a stairway that had a very deep storage area built into the walls, where everything was stored in sections: olive oil, *tahenah*, couscous, beans, wheat, sugar, rice, dried tomatoes, different kinds of jams, and different kinds of juice, because there were many orchards in Gaza. When I say store, or speak about rice or sugar, I am speaking of quantities of very big sacks, not like today where people buy by the kilo. They were stored for the year, and some villages still use this type of storage area. We used to grind the wheat and beans with a hand-operated rock mill. This rock mill consisted of two very heavy stones on top of each other. The top rock had a hole in the middle where the grains would be dropped in, and there was a handle that we turned to grind the grains between the rocks. Some people even now still use these stones.

We lived in a small house beside my grandfather's sesame press and we could smell the sesame, which has a lovely aroma. I still remember when we were young, taking the sesame oil and red *tahenah* and sharing it with the neighbourhood. In the yard of our home was a covered water cistern made of ceramic tiles, with a fountain in the middle. It stored water and wasn't very deep, about 1 or 2 metres, and a square metre in width. During winter, water wasn't a problem because

Sahbaa (on the right) with her mother and siblings, Gaza, 1940s.
(Photo courtesy of Sahbaa's family)

of the rain, and we collected rainwater in pots to fill the cistern. We used it when we needed it. Sometimes there were droughts during those years and there were no taps at home, so every home had a small cistern like this in the centre of the home. In summer, we would buy from a man who filled the cistern with water that he brought in goatskins, so we could use it when necessary for washing, bathing, and cleaning. This man filled his goatskins with water from a well in Sheikh 'Ejleen and would go around selling it, but some houses stored rainwater for their daily needs and did not need to buy it. There was another well called Al Sheikh Hassan, close to the beach, which sold to that area; it would supply water to those living there as well as to Gazans vacationing on the beach during the summer. When we were young, we had to clean the bottom of our cistern, which consisted of a lot of scrubbing and rinsing so that the water would not get contaminated. Later, pipes were installed.

Then in about 1944, we rented our home to people in Al Daraj and moved to Al Sabra, which was a new suburb with more modern houses. They had water taps and even bathtubs inside; almost everything was like nowadays. My mother was very elegant, had many friends, and didn't want to spend all her life in Al Daraj, so we were all happy when we rented this new house in Al Sabra, which was also closer to our school. She had a reception day every month, on Thursday, when her women friends got together for a visit and enjoyed themselves. They wore their best dresses, put on makeup, and had their hair done and dyed with henna. We were young and not allowed to join them, so we went to the Baladiyah park (a public park) and played.

In 1967 when Israel occupied Gaza, they destroyed many beautiful houses, among them the houses where my uncles and aunts lived, and they began widening the streets for their security purposes. This was the policy of General Ariel Sharon, then the commander of the southern area, to increase control in Gaza and guarantee easy access for military jeeps and vehicles to commute through the streets. They did this in order to supress and arrest the *Fedayeen* and the activists. It was then that my grandfather's house was demolished and a new one was built, which my aunt now rents out to families. I wasn't there when the house was destroyed so I don't know the details, but when I returned to Gaza, I was astonished because everything was completely changed. I saw the new Al Wehda Street and was deeply saddened because the house in which we grew up and had many childhood memories was gone and now became just that: a childhood memory.

Every morning, we greeted my grandfather and kissed his hand, and he gave us one *qersh* (Palestinian *piaster*). We had Palestinian currency then, as well as Palestinian stamps and Palestinian passports issued by the British Mandate. The British Mandate administered Gaza, and every four years a district commissioner would come with his family to live here. Then they would move to other areas like Nablus or Haifa because Palestine was divided into sixteen districts.[2] The commissioner was the connection between the Mandate and the people, and he solved their problems with the British, especially if someone had a relative in the English prison or there were problems concerning the *Fedayeen*, or any other troubles at the district level. He was a mediator, like the governor or mayor nowadays, and was regularly moved so he wouldn't develop relationships with people that could later become a threat to the Mandate. There were Palestinians who invited these officials to their homes and fields for social occasions like weddings and celebrations— and while some Palestinians might have advanced their interests with the colonizers, for the most part, it was genuine and pure Arab generosity. Many officials were sad when they left Gaza because the people were very kind, humble, and forgiving, even though Gaza was the southern agricultural zone and considered one of the poorest areas in Palestine. I remember groups of British and Australian soldiers used to come and go. We saw them sometimes passing through Gaza on their way to Egypt, and some of them were black or very dark brown.[3] As children we were afraid of soldiers, so we used to flee whenever we saw them.

The British Mandate had centres in many places, and in Gaza it was Al Saraya that was the centre for the British army.[4] The building in front of it, what we now call the Abu

Sahbaa at home, Gaza, 1940s. (Photo courtesy of Sahbaa's family)

Khadra building, was the headquarters of the international observers when they came to Gaza in 1957 to monitor the situation after the Israeli withdrawal in the aftermath of the 1956 invasion.[5] During the 1930s and 1940s, all the area from Al Saraya, the centre of Gaza City, to the sea was big empty hills of sand that separated Gaza City from the beach. We passed Al Saraya on our way to the beach on donkeys, or sometimes in taxis, but there were very few taxis then.

This is the extent of what I remember of back then as I was young at the time, but I remember a cousin of my father who lived in Al Majdal town, which is about 20 kilometres from Gaza, who was active with the *Fedayeen*. He was caught by the British soldiers and imprisoned for five years because he had a gun, and when he was released, I went with my father to welcome him. This was during the 1940s. Having a weapon was forbidden by the British because they didn't want us to defend ourselves against them or the Zionist militias; they were causing many problems for the Palestinians and taking over our land by building small colonies and military posts, which they would then slowly expand from. So, whoever the British caught possessing a weapon, or even a knife, would be sent directly to prison—sometimes for a very long time.

I remember some demonstrations protesting the British policies in Palestine, but I am not sure of the specific reasons for the ones I witnessed. In 1936, there were many problems with the British and many demonstrations against them, but I only vaguely remember groups of people chanting in the streets of Gaza.[6] Later, I learned from researching and reading that there was a six-month strike that was part of the Arab revolt, in which transportation and the movement of goods were stopped. People were protesting the British policies that allowed tens of thousands of Jews to immigrate to Palestine, as they felt the threat of this influx of foreigners who were taking over our land. In Gaza, like everywhere else, committees and groups were created to protest and fight the British. Some people in Gaza even stopped buying through the English, boycotting their businesses, and cutting any ties with them.

We used to visit and play outside with the neighbours' children. We played marbles, went to the sea, and made our own toys such as *arayis* (bridal dolls). We drew the outline

of the doll on material, then cut, sewed, and stuffed it with
other material or whatever we had. We made her hair from
cotton or wool thread and drew two eyes and eyebrows, a
nose, and a mouth, and made different outfits for them.
We also flew colourful kites that we made during school
vacation in the summer. We had competitions to see who
could make the most beautiful kite and who could fly their
kite the highest, and sometimes there were problems when
the strings would get tangled. We flew our kites close to the
sesame press because there was a wide, empty area where
they could fly free, and when we moved to Al Sabra, we flew
them from the roof of our house. We also went to the cinema
and the current Baladiyah park, close to the Al Saraya centre,
especially during the three-month summer vacation. I have
very nice memories of that time. There were three cinemas
in Gaza then and they were segregated: one side for men
and the other for women. We went every Friday with our
family or friends to see Arabic films, mostly Egyptian ones.
I wonder now how we are in the twenty-first century and
don't even have a cinema here, but we did in the 1930s and
1940s, maybe even before then. Once when I was very young,
my mother took me to the Al Hamra cinema in Jaffa.[7] I don't
remember much of what I saw, but I remember the feeling
of being taken aback with the beauty of Jaffa. We sometimes
read small stories, but not much because we were tired
after studying for exams, so during the summer holidays
we played, went to Gaza beach, and helped our mothers
and neighbours, and everyone had a special job. The social
fabric of Gaza then was very strong, and people helped each
other. I can say that this is still the norm in Gaza, despite the
passage of years.

My job was helping my mother bake bread, and like most people, I took the dough to an oven in Al Daraj for the baker to bake. Some people in Gaza City had a clay oven in their home so they baked the bread themselves. But most people used the bakers' ovens, which were always situated in close proximity to people's homes. In Al Sabra, a boy came and collected our dough for the oven, and we paid him. We also sent spinach bread, thyme bread, meat covered with dough, and *ka'k al 'Eid* (*'Eid* biscuits) to be baked in the oven. It was not like today, where people can cook in their own ovens or buy them ready-made; this was what we did then. Usually, old ladies made *ka'k al 'Eid* and we helped by sprinkling icing sugar on them after they were baked. Then we stored them in big containers in layers so they wouldn't break. Guests were offered *ka'k* when they came at night, and all through Ramadan you could smell *ka'k* everywhere as they cooked. We exchanged with each other to see whose tasted the best. To this day, people still keep this tradition and do these taste tests of each other's cooking.

We bought clothes for *'Eid* (the celebration of feast after the holy month of Ramadan) from Jaffa. My mother bought socks and shoes and new dresses, and sometimes made the dresses herself because she was talented and skilled at sewing. Then we ironed and wrapped them, and sometimes laid them flat under the mattress, and waited for the morning to celebrate. On the morning of the feast, we shook hands and then kissed the hands of my grandfather and father before they gave us the *'Eidiyyeh* (money given to children on *'Eid* day), a custom of the feast.

During most of the summer it was so hot in the houses and there were no air conditioners or refrigerators, so Gazan people went to the beach. We usually walked or rode donkeys

or horses, and many families owned animals that they used
for local transportation. We took food, drinks, clothes, and
tents, and stayed for the three months of summer vacation.
And from time to time we checked in on our houses. The
weather was different then, with cold, rainy winters and hot
summers, unlike the dry winters of these days.

My mother used to take us to Hammam Al Samra in
Gaza's Old City.[8] It was the time to relax from the whole
week for ladies, and they made appointments with each
other to go there or went in groups with their neighbours,
so the bath was usually crowded. It was a social event where
women met, laughed, gossiped, and enjoyed their time. We
were young and listened to their stories, jokes, and chatter,
and overall just enjoyed the atmosphere. We carried our
clothes, combs, perfume, towels, and a special thick black
soap of pure olive oil imported from Syria in a special bag
called a *buqja*, which came from Turkey. It was made of
velvet and covered with silk or gold embroidery, like a
cushion cover, and was made especially for baths. People
carried these bags to show that they were rich. Even now
if you go to the old houses, you will see these bags hanging
on the walls as antiques. When we entered the Hammam,
we put the *buqja* in the first room and changed our clothes
and then entered the steam-filled bath. In the middle of the
bath was a fountain with hot and cold water taps, where our
mothers washed our bodies and washed and combed our
hair as the water streamed off us. There were also special
lady masseurs. It was really fun, and we enjoyed ourselves.
I think there was another Turkish bath called Hammam Al
Wazeer, but I don't exactly know where. In Tunis and other
Arab countries, many of these public baths still exist, and
they are still called Turkish Baths and many people go there.

Hammam Al Samra has now been restored as part of our local heritage and has started to function again in Gaza.

At that time, 'Omar Al Mukhtar was a big asphalt street with many green spaces and big shops.[9] There were two big bookshops owned by the Hekmat Barzaq and Khamis Abu Sha'ban families, which sold all kinds of literature and books from Lebanon, Egypt, Syria, and other countries. I still remember the Abu Rahma family, which was famous for importing and selling cloth from Turkey and China. Women went from house to house selling it. My grandfather would shop for us at a big market on the current Fahmi Beik Street in Gaza's Old City, and if he forgot something, he sent us children or sometimes one of the workers from the sesame press to get it. We also bought other things from mobile vendors who would pass by our house on carts, calling out whatever they were selling. This included things like fresh bread and milk, fruits and vegetables, gas, and aluminum, etc., which eliminated the need for us to go to the shops or market for these things.

All Palestinian families in Gaza City sent their children to school, and it was normal for girls to go to school. I used to meet my friends and we would walk together in a group. We were taught by very good local teachers who had graduated from the teachers' training college in Ramallah. When my sisters became older, they continued their education at Schmidt College in Jerusalem because there were no high schools for girls in Gaza then. My oldest sister and aunts were among the first from Gaza to study at Schmidt College, and my aunt, Yusra Al-Barbari, was the first student from Gaza to attend Cairo University, where she studied history. She then became a headmistress, and later the head of the Women's Union in Palestine.[10] There was also a teachers' college in Jerusalem from which another aunt of mine grad-uated. My older brother went to Gaza College, a private high school for boys, and then continued his studies in Egypt. My younger brother was too young to attend schools when we were in Gaza, so his schooling and education were in Egypt.

The education system followed the British system and the matriculation was equal to *tawjihi*. Every district in Palestine had its own administration centre, with headmasters, inspectors, and administrators. The school curriculum was designed in the education office based in Jerusalem, where our school certificates were stamped with a Palestinian stamp. Palestinian inspectors were well educated in Cairo and Beirut, and they came from different parts of Palestine to supervise the teachers and the schools. Our education was very strong, and even now I remember very well what we studied as part of the curriculum. We studied the books of Mustafa Al Dabagh, a renowned Palestinian historian and instructor who came to the schools to supervise the teachers in history and geography. We also studied cooking, domestic science, embroidery, and sewing. We were taught to paint and use our hands, but we weren't encouraged to read books outside of school. I don't ever remember there being a library, or us exchanging books in school. The only books we read at school were from the curriculum, which we had to study for exams. In the last year, we studied religion and those classes were separated: Muslim girls studied the Islamic religion, while the Christian girls studied theirs. We read, studied, memorized, and recited verses of the holy Quran, and during these lessons we wore white dresses and white socks, and covered our heads with white handkerchiefs.

Usually we dressed however we wanted, and nobody was forced to wear anything in particular. We enjoyed our freedom in everything. Very few women wore veils except old ladies. My oldest uncle, Kamal, understood religion very well and never forced us to wear the veil, long sleeves, or long skirts, or pray, or do anything against our will. He was a great lawyer with an open mind and heart with very good manners and values. He studied at the American University in Cairo and later in Beirut, and after he obtained his legal licence from the Law College in Jerusalem he worked in the courts in Gaza and all over Palestine. We lost my Uncle Kamal in 1967 when he went to the mosque to pray the morning prayer during a curfew. For a week people weren't allowed out of their houses, and after the curfew was lifted everybody searched for missing family members. Many bodies lay everywhere in the streets that had become so bloated that they were unrecognizable, so people hurried to bury them. My family searched everywhere, but they couldn't find my uncle and we don't know what happened to him. I was in Syria then, but we were informed later of his passing. It was a great loss for my family and the community in Gaza. We mourned him for a very long time.

Israel committed many crimes against Palestinians; they even buried people alive. Yes, in 1967, people saw the Israeli soldiers bury Palestinians and Egyptian soldiers alive, after they had been captured or had surrendered, and then they collected the dead bodies together to hide their crimes.[11] They did a similar thing during the first *Intifada* when they ordered young Palestinian men from a village in the West Bank to lie down and then dumped sand over their bodies using a bulldozer. By a miracle some people saw the soldiers, and right after the army left the people dug them out and took them to the hospital.[12] In 1967, as was the case in 1956, Israel committed many horrible crimes during the curfews it imposed on the Strip, like they did in the Jenin massacre in 2002, when they closed the refugee camp and massacred dozens of civilians and demolished their homes and shops, rendering hundreds of families homeless.[13] Three or four years ago, when municipality workers were digging the sewage system beside the park in Gaza, they found many bones and skulls and knew they were from 1967 because there was a massacre here in Gaza City, and many people were lost at that time. Still now, we don't know whether my uncle was killed, buried dead, or buried alive, but what we do know is that he is no longer with us.

I had three uncles, and I told you about one. Another went to Turkey and then to America, where he studied engineering in 1942, and another continued his studies in California after he finished at the Khadori Agricultural College in Palestine. It was not just my uncles, but many, many Palestinian families sent their sons abroad to study. Palestinians studied in Britain, America, Turkey, Cairo, and Beirut. We are an educated nation that cares enough to send our children to study outside or abroad—unlike what Israel tries to promote to the world, that we are uncivilized people.

During the 1940s, electricity came to Gaza for the first time, and when the municipality lit the streets there was a big celebration. Before this, a man would go around and light up the streets with kerosene lamps at a certain time of night, and in the morning the light was extinguished. We also used kerosene lamps at home. We studied by these lamps; I don't remember that my mother ever had to urge us to study, unlike with children nowadays. We didn't have private tutors, but instead studied by ourselves before we played.

Sahbaa at school, Gaza, 1940s. (Photo courtesy of Sahbaa's family)

Merchants travelled to Turkey and brought back special lamps called *fawanees*, with beautiful different-coloured glass in gold patterns. I still have a big one that my mother-in-law gave us for our wedding that had belonged to her mother.

The farthest parts of Palestine I had been to before 1948 were Al Majdal, Isdud, and Jaffa, and I also had gone to the town of Khan Younis in the southern part of the Strip, where my sisters and aunts taught. I had never visited Jerusalem then. When I was five years old, I went to Cairo to have my eyes treated, but I don't remember much of the trip. My mother's family lived in Cairo and owned the famous Halawa factories, which produced cotton cloth. We travelled by train to Egypt then, but during the 1948 war, Israel destroyed the railway. During the 1956 attack on Gaza, they targeted and destroyed the railway again, as well as the bridge that crossed the Suez Canal. This policy of targeting Palestinian infrastructure and homes is still going on. A few months ago, the Israeli F16 planes hit the Al Saraya building during working hours, leaving many casualities and a lot of destruction. Last month, they dropped a one-ton bomb on Al Daraj, my old neighbourhood. Fourteen people were killed, and among them were nine children. A large number of people were wounded in the attack, too. Probably hundreds, as the place is very crowded, but I don't remember the exact number. I felt my heart stopping when I was watching the stories of the survivors in the news.[14] What crime did those children commit to be slaughtered in the middle of night in this barbaric way?

2 / The 1948 *Nakba* and Studies in Cairo

IN 1947, we read in the newspapers about the clashes of the far-off places in north Palestine, when the Haganah and Irgun Zionist militias began planning to take over the towns adjacent to them. I didn't understand what was going on then, but I remember my family following the news in the newspapers and trying to get information from people who were visiting Gaza from Jerusalem and Jaffa. I had never heard about these militia in Gaza, and perhaps all that I can remember of them was the talk about their colonies and the problems that they caused for Palestinians. I heard about the Rehovot colony from my father, who travelled a lot to Jaffa and the north.

My mother, our neighbours, and other women helped the influx of refugees, numbering over two hundred thousand, almost four times the population of the Strip then. They were mostly peasants and landowners who suddenly ended up in the streets after being forced out of their homes and off their lands in 1948. They lost everything and became home-less. They were everywhere and could be spotted in any of Gaza's corners. Many of these refugees had nothing, literally nothing, as they were fleeing for their lives, and they were probably thinking that they wouldn't stay that long before they could return home. The Gazan women sewed *jalabiyaat* and also dresses for the women and for their children, or helped by giving clothes, bandages, shelter if they could, and food. When I became older, I realized that these women may have made a big mistake, that instead they should have urged these refugees to go back to their homes, no matter the cost, and not surrender to these gangs and become refugees. If they had walked back in masses, they might have forced Israel to open the borders and let them back. Who knows? The United Nations and the American Friends Service Committee, the Quakers, should have also insisted on this and assisted in their return by forcing Israel to implement the UN Resolution 194 of 1948, which granted refugees the right to return,[1] rather than giving help with milk, cans of food, and second-hand clothes. Helping Palestinian refugees by merely giving them some old clothes and a little food only helped Israel turn its back on the UN resolutions. In my opinion, the UN complicated the issue of refugees by taking on the burden that Israel should have dealt with. Now, after over half a century, Israel even tries to escape from the responsibility of causing the *Nakba* (the catastrophe of dispossession) in the first place, and still refuses to implement Resolution 194. I wonder what the advantage is of issuing UN resolutions without implementing them.

Most Palestinian families, especially after the *Nakba*, were helped by their husbands, fathers, and sons who worked outside of Palestine, especially in the rich Gulf countries such as Saudi Arabia, Kuwait, and the United Arab Emirates. They sent money and carried the responsibility for their families on their shoulders.[2] They returned every year or two for a short holiday, while the wives and mothers took responsibility for everything at home, including raising the children and helping them with their studies. Many families had also lost husbands and sons in the wars and the wives had to take on all the responsibility. The economic situation in Gaza was very difficult because the majority of Palestinians lost their property and land during the war; the Indigenous people of Gaza lost their means of livelihood and the larger markets in Palestine where they used to buy and sell their goods. This is all in addition to the restrictions imposed on their freedom of movement and the continuous attacks on Gaza after the *Nakba*.

All educated Palestinians went to work, especially to teach, in Kuwait, Saudi Arabia, and other rich Gulf countries to help in financially supporting their families. After the 1948 war there was no work as Gaza is very small, with limited resources and capacity to absorb the huge number of people who ended up in the Strip. So Palestinian refugees began going to the Arab countries to work, to make a living, and to invest in educating the next generation. In fact, there is no other way open for Palestinians except through education. Their certificates are their tools to a better future, and this is the only way that is open for them to obtain work outside. It not only helps the individual but also the family, who suffer and sacrifice a lot for the next generation to be educated. After the war, the society was very strong and families stood together. Women of the *Nakba* generation were the cornerstones and generally responsible for raising the next generations. I would say that the *Nakba* generation was the strongest generation.

I couldn't finish high school on time because of the 1948 war. My father contracted stomach cancer and was broken-hearted as a result of his health, the war, and the problems of work and the restrictions. At the beginning of 1949, he became so sick that my mother and family went with him for treatment in Cairo, where my brother started and finished high school. I stayed in Gaza because I was already in my last year of high school.

My father died in Cairo in 1950 while I was in Gaza, and the responsibility for raising us was heavy on my mother and two older sisters. My mother became a father, a mother, and a friend all in one. My oldest sister helped us financially from Kuwait, where she worked as a teacher, and my second sister learned sewing and high fashion in Cairo and helped raise us. In fact, my two sisters helped the family get on its feet again, and I received my tertiary degree with their help. My mother stayed in Egypt after my father died because her family was there. The situation in Gaza had changed after the *Nakba*, and so there was, for my mother, both the loss of her homeland and the loss of my father, and subsequently no real reason for her to return. Also, the younger children were starting school, and my brother was ready for *tawjihi*. At that time, students had to be physically present for their *tawjihi* exams in Egypt. After the 1948 *Nakba*, the Gaza Strip was administered by Egypt, and a few years later, they allowed the high schools in Gaza to give *tawjihi* exams under the supervision of the Egyptian officials. So, students could sit for their examinations in Gaza without the hassle of travelling to Egypt. I stayed in Gaza at my grandfather's house with my sister, who was a teacher in Khan Younis, for just over a year to finish my schooling. When I was seventeen years old, I joined my family in Cairo, where I had to repeat my final year of high school. I had a friend there who was the same age and in the same class who liked reading, and we exchanged books. She introduced me to many Arab writers,

and from that time I began the habit of reading to expand
my knowledge.

There was a big difference between life in Egypt and Gaza,
and living in Egypt had a big impact on my character and my
life. In Egypt, there were big wide streets, huge buildings,
many universities and schools, shops, cinemas, bookstores,
and theatres. Cairo was a very big city compared to tiny Gaza
City. There, you felt the real meaning of life compared to
the narrow outlook you get from being in Gaza. We had good
relationships with our neighbours in Egypt and often visited
each other. During some vacations we travelled back to Gaza,
but most of the time our aunts came to visit us because it
was a good opportunity for them to see Egypt—unlike these
days, it was easy to travel there then. I also remember how
happy we were when my sister came from Kuwait during her
vacations, bringing many gifts of nice clothes, watches, and
toys. While in Kuwait, she studied English through distance
education, so she came twice a year to sit for her exams
and take a break from her work. She was studying for her
Bachelor of Arts in English.

In Gaza, my brother had belonged to the Boy Scouts and
went with his teachers on camping trips to Jerash and Petra
in Jordan.[3] There was nothing for girls in Gaza then, but I
joined the Girl Guides during secondary school in Cairo.
I went on camping trips to southern Egypt, to Aswan and
Luxor. One year we went to Marsa Matruh, a beautiful beach
area in Egypt. At camp, we folded our mattresses, washed our
clothes, cleaned the campground, helped prepare the food,
and did physical education. At night, we grilled food on the
fire, and we sang and danced with our teachers and friends.
During the day, we went to see the antiquities in Karnak
and went on tours on the Nile. The camp lasted for two

weeks during the summer vacation because this was the only opportunity to visit faraway places. We played volleyball and racquetball on the beach and became very tanned. I learned to swim there. It was a wonderful time that I enjoyed very much and still remember vividly.

When I was at Cairo University, I went for a two-day trip to Al Ghardaqa on the Red Sea, and at that time it was an untouched area and a very big, beautiful, and clean place. We swam in the sea and even saw coral. Fifteen boys and girls went—not a large number because there were not a lot of open-minded people then, so not many families allowed their daughters to go on mixed trips. I went because we were educated and raised with no difference between boys and girls, so we were allowed to go on these trips. My mother was open-minded and encouraged us to participate in these groups because she knew their advantages. She believed that a confident girl can protect herself from anything, and that manners that are planted and grow within you protect you from doing anything bad or causing any wrongdoing.

When my brother started university, he embraced the local culture of music, history, Arabic and international literature, books, and films, which influenced him very much. He liked reading and had a big library that contained many books, and this was reflected in me. I read many Egyptian writers such as Najib Mahfouz, who won the Nobel prize for literature, and the well-known novelist and journalist Ihsan Abdel Quddous. My brother also loved classical music, and through him I came to know the music of Beethoven, Mozart, and others. He took us to the cinema, Umm Kulthum[4] concerts, and parties, and I saw many dance groups from Eastern Europe and popular groups from China perform in Egypt.[5] When he left Egypt, I continued taking my younger brother and sisters to these shows, and later, at university, I listened to an hour of classical music every Monday afternoon, which was organized by the Dean of the Arts College of Cairo University. This atmosphere shaped my character, and I became a member on many cultural and arts committees that raised the awareness of different cultures.

Before the *Nakba* there were three powers in Egypt: the King, the British, and Al Wafd (Al Wafd Party), a very strong and popular nationalist party supported by the Egyptians. King Farouk was against this party and imprisoned its leader until the British Ambassador forced him to release him. After 1948, people raised many questions about the *Nakba*, and many nationalist movements and groups were formed that searched for answers about how Palestine was lost and why the Egyptian government did not win the war. At the same time, their defeat in Palestine had its effect on the Egyptian military because it had been sold defective and old weapons that backfired and killed many of the Egyptian soldiers. The British had their headquarters situated on a big piece of land in Cairo called Al Tahrir Square, where the Nile Hilton Hotel is now. There were also many British bases and barracks in the towns of Isma'elia and Suez. In 1951, the British shot and killed many Egyptian policemen in Isma'elia, which led to demonstrations all over Egypt against the British and the King. People were also very angry about the defeat in Palestine, the defective weapons, and the siege of the Egyptian army in the village of Al Faluja in Palestine. Abd Al Nasser, a commander of a large unit of the Egyptian army, was trapped in that strategic village together with his troops and surrounded by Israeli forces for a long time. The siege lasted from October 1948 until February 1949 and ended when an agreement was reached. Abd Al

Nasser withdrew with his unit and returned to Egypt.[6] Israel then occupied Al Faluja and expelled its people. The humiliation of the Egyptian army in the village and the defeat in Palestine immensely influenced the situation in Egypt and accelerated anger against the King and the British, so a group from the army called the Free Officers planned to change the regime and get rid of the King and the British altogether.

The year 1952 was an eventful year in which many things happened. Cairo, which was a very beautiful city and considered the capital of all the Arab countries, was going into turmoil. In January 1952, many cinemas and big stores were burned, and many Egyptian businessmen sent all their money outside of Egypt, which hit the economy hard. I was in high school at the time, and from our home, I saw the burning of Cairo from the late afternoon into the night, accompanied by the sounds of explosions from all directions.[7] I remember there were demonstrations against the King and his alliance to the British that same night and the day after, but I didn't participate. Many newspapers that wrote against the King and his rule were temporarily shut down.

King Farouk imposed martial law, with curfews and people being arrested for any and even no reason. He abolished many parties, national movements, elections, and newspapers, and banned demonstrations, and just like that, the ministers were changed one after another. The King needed to keep the British in Egypt to protect his rule because the situation was unstable. The Egyptian Prime Minister Mahmoud Noqrashi Pasha was assassinated in 1948 as he left parliament as well as another Egyptian minister, both because they had cooperated with the British. A British Consul was also assassinated in that period. The Muslim Brotherhood was accused, and many Egyptians were arrested. There were also earlier demonstrations that took place in which university students participated, and many were killed during one of those, when the British soldiers opened fire on the students and opened up the bridge under their feet. This was called the Abbas Bridge Massacre of 1946.[8] At the same time, the nationalist movement, Muslim Brotherhood, and communist parties grew stronger.

A large group inside the army was against the weakness and corruption of the government regarding their lack of support for the Palestinian cause. They were also against Farouk's corrupt regime and his collusion with the British colonizers. Abd Al Nasser was an army captain under siege in Al Faluja during the 1948 war. Three years later in Cairo, led by Mohammed Najib and Abd Al Nasser, the group called the Free Officers made the arrangements necessary to take power. On July 23, 1952, the Free Officers group went to the radio station at the palace and placed the ministers under house arrest before taking over the ministries.[9] Three days later, the King was ordered to leave and went by yacht from Alexandria to Rome.

So, Egypt changed from a monarchy to a republic due to a group of Egyptian army officers who were supported by the people. The rich and influential Egyptian elite were very angry. Some were put under house arrest and under guard. We heard the news on the radio and in the newspapers, that the army had occupied the palace, and the next day we saw pictures of the new leaders in the newspapers and read about their plans. As Palestinians, we considered this revolution as revenge against the corruption of the King and the treason of the British who had caused our defeat back home, and also as retaliation for the defeat of the Egyptian army in 1948. Egyptians were happy and took to the streets to demonstrate

in support of this revolution and the new leaders; they were
ready to leave behind the reign of the corrupt King and
his ministers, and rid the country of the poverty, diseases,
oppression, and injustice that had come as a result. If there
had not been overwhelming support by the people, they
never would have succeeded in laying siege to the palace
because it was such a small group.

Abd Al Nasser did many good things for Egypt. He nationalized the textile industry and all the factories in Cairo
belonging to the rich people, and he created many industrial
projects using stainless steel and iron and established hundreds
of factories that gave work to tens of thousands of Egyptians.
He instituted agricultural reform, where he took land from
the rich that owned the majority and distributed it among
the farmers who had previously worked as slaves on their
land, so that everybody owned only two hectares. He developed the education system and made it free for all children
in all schools; this was especially good for the children of
farmers, who couldn't afford to pay for education. He developed the hospitals and allowed birth control and opened up
the universities, but one of his greatest achievements was
making university education free for Palestinians. He built
the high dam and nationalized the Suez Canal—projects that
improved the economic situation for the people of Egypt.
To this day, people still remember his many projects to help
poor people, especially the land reform, unlike President
Sadat, who succeeded him and did little for the people.[10]

The time I spent in Cairo was one of the best times of my
life. It was a time of nationalism because Abd Al Nasser was
president, and his special concern, which he always spoke
about, was the nationalist problem in the Arab countries and
his dream to unite all of them together. When we listened

to his speeches, we felt the glory, the pride, and the unity of Arabs from the Atlantic Ocean to the Arab Gulf. I can call that time the high tide of nationalism, and now we are living at its low ebb. I wish my children had lived then, because being born and raised at that time created a special and strong individual character that took pride and appreciation in being Arab. Now we are living in a time where there is lots of blood, lots of martyrs, lots of tragedies, and lots of massacres every day, and nobody moves a centimetre.

In 1953, I began studying philosophy and psychology at Cairo University, and I graduated in January 1958. I was also an active member of the Palestinian Students' Association, led by Yasser Arafat, with people from the Communist Party, Muslim Brotherhood, Ba'th Party, and Nationalist Party; there were many political parties. All the members of the future Palestinian leadership—Yasser Arafat, Abu Iyad, Abu Al Adeeb, and Abu Lutof—were university students at that time. When I attended the Palestinian Students' Association, I was attracted to the Marxists' ideas that explain and expose our world problems of inequality, poverty, and oppression, and venues for human liberation. For me, their ideas and discourse were rational, deep, and of a very high standard. There were always confrontations between the parties that ended in fistfights, but the communists only ever fought with words. I found that the Marxist students had good manners, a good reputation, and cared about community relations and about humanity, and subsequently I became interested in their ideas and approaches. I started reading more books on Marxism and started to value their principles and ideas, especially those on power and class relations, colonialism, imperialism, and exploitation of the working class. I thought that if their ideas and approaches to our world problems were implemented, especially in our part of the world, they could make a huge difference and help to provide a dignified life and a good future. I found Marxists open-minded and not rigid in their thinking. They liked to read and learn and understand and analyze. Their ideology was not only for Palestine. It was universal and was inclusive of all people—the poor, the oppressed, the marginalized, and the excluded. It was for justice, and against colonization and apartheid. We supported South Africa in its struggle for freedom and against the racial discrimination experienced by the black South African people and the exploitation of the apartheid regime. We were on the side of all oppressed people in their struggle for dignity and freedom, wherever they were. The communists were united with the nationalist party, the Muslim Brotherhood, and the Ba'th Party in opposing the Johnson proposal to re-settle Palestinian refugees in the Sinai Desert, as well as the Eisenhower Doctrine, which wanted the Arab countries to be under the American umbrella against the Soviet Union.[11] I liked the way the communist party united all the different parties to oppose those colonial and imperial proposals.

In 1954, there were clashes against Abd Al Nasser because he had not fulfilled his promises of democracy, and had banned all Islamic, communist, Ba'thist, and nationalist parties. Many Palestinian students were members of these parties and everybody knew of them, but if the government discovered this, they were always harassed because it was illegal. I remember always being followed by Egyptian Intelligence on buses, at the university, while shopping, on the street—everywhere in Cairo. Members of the different parties were to some extent free to write what they thought

Sahbaa with her aunt, Yusra (back row, right), the founding President of the Palestinian Women's Union in Gaza, on a school trip to Port Saeed, Egypt, 1957. (Photo courtesy of Sahbaa's family)

in many newspapers, but if they formed groups to express their opinions or plan activities, they were arrested.

Cairo was my favourite place because my family was there, and I also lived the most active years of my life there. I lived through the best of the nationalist movement years in that city, and in spite of the harassment I really enjoyed it and benefited immensely while living in Cairo. It was the most important period of struggle for me. Cairo taught me how to discuss, listen, respond, and be open-minded; I was able to attend many conferences, festivals, meetings, and lectures that formed my character. This is why I always believe that working together in groups or teams increases one's abilities, making the individual forget the self, while being part of a collective. You learn through these interactions, how to agree and disagree, to speak and to listen, and to respect the opinions and views of others. By doing so, you also learn to care by being empathetic to the situation and sympathetic to the problems and suffering. This is why I always encouraged my students to be involved in activities, groups, and initiatives, whether social or political, because through these activities we can continue to learn and grow.

I visited many countries, and that started when I was first a student. In 1956, I was one of five students chosen as a member of a delegation for a conference called Youth, Friendship and Peace that was held in Warsaw. Among the five chosen students was Yasser Arafat (who would later become the head of the Palestine Liberation Organization, or PLO). I went by ship from Alexandria to Italy, then by train to Austria, where I still remember the Alps and the beautiful scenery, after which we crossed Czechoslovakia by train (which was then part of the Eastern Bloc). There were many problems for Palestinians in obtaining visas to go through these various borders. This experience of travelling abroad helped me to understand much of the outside world, and the meaning of freedom and value of human rights. There were many students from colonized countries such as South Africa, Latin America, and the Arab world, as well as Marxists and nationalists who had problems within their regimes. They all participated and shared their concerns with one another at the conference, which was also refreshing for us as a collective to see.

On my way back, I was prevented from entering Syria because my Egyptian residence permit stamped on my travel document had expired. At that time, between 1948 and 1967,

Gaza was under the Egyptian administration, which was the body that issued travel documents. So, I was forced to return to Romania on the same ship and then go on to Budapest, where I stayed for two weeks until a Lebanese comrade acquired tickets through the international students' union for me and another three men to travel to Istanbul. While we waited, we were taken every day to see the museums, gardens, and parks of Romania. Our guide was a member of the International Youth Union and he did his best to solve our problems and let us enjoy our time. In fact, I was greatly helped by the conference participants and the organizers while I was stuck between the borders, especially by their advice about where to go and which offices to ask for help. Honestly, I didn't feel worried or afraid. I knew that the conference organizers had dealt with those kinds of problems, so they would find a solution to our problem and return us safely home to our families. Many years later, one of them was very happy and surprised when he met my son by accident in Germany.

In Istanbul, the Egyptian Consul was very understanding and helped me obtain permission to enter Egypt with my expired residence permit, and I flew from there to Cairo. I was worried about losing this permit and also about my university studies because it was my final year and the academic year had already started in Cairo. Instead of one month away, I had spent three months from July to September travelling by land, sea, and air. To this day, I truly appreciate and value the understanding and the help offered to me by several eastern European countries that stood by me until my problem was solved. I also appreciated the role of the Egyptian embassy at that time. I have great respect for Egypt, which helped Palestinians in many different ways: its borders were usually kept open for us, it gave us residence permits, we acquired free higher education there, and some even found work.

My mother didn't know about these problems and thought I had been invited to attend conferences in other countries, and after I returned, I told her what had happened. If Yasser Arafat had known, he probably would have tried his best to solve my problem because he was the head of our delegation, but while we were in Warsaw, another conference was held under the umbrella of the International Students' Union and he went to represent the Palestinians. After this experience, I understood when Mu'in Bseiso, the Palestinian poet and author, who later became my husband, wrote about the suffering of Palestinians at airports, harbours, and train stations. I was able to better understand the Palestinian tragedy that culminated in us losing our homeland and becoming stateless, which means that we physically exist and at the same time do not exist, because we are stateless and possess no recognized documents. Before that experience, I did not appreciate the exact meaning of not having an identity card or recognized document or passport, but when I started to travel and ended up stranded in airports, I knew exactly what it meant for Palestinians not to have it.

When I returned to Cairo in September 1956, I continued my studies. Two months after my return, in November 1956, Israel, Britain, and France attacked Egypt. Some students went to the front to fight, and we demonstrated in support of Abd Al Nasser's government. Every day, the first university lecture was a news update on the war, and people followed the news on the radio everywhere. We put blue adhesive plastic on the windows to hide the light, and I remember that when we heard the sirens warning of attacks on Cairo, we turned off the lights and went down and gathered with

other people. I attended a nursing and first aid course in
a hospital, and I also took a self-defence course in a closed
camp with other students; these courses were to prepare
us for emergencies, so that we could help in emergency
situations and in hospitals. I was active in different community associations, and was a member of an association that
organized many demonstrations and strikes and that also
collected and distributed assistance among needy people.
This association's greatest achievement was its cooperation
with the Egyptian government, resulting in financial assistance of seven Egyptian pounds per month for Palestinian
students from Gaza whose parents were affected by the war.

When Mu'in was a student, he submitted poems to
magazines and newspapers and wrote historical plays for
the Voice of Palestine Radio in Cairo. I first got to know
about him through my brother, who read his poems. I
read his work in magazines and books and I liked Mu'in's
poems very much. The first time I met him was in jail. He
was imprisoned together with many community leaders
and activists who went into the streets of Gaza to protest
against Johnson's plan, which proposed settling Palestinian
refugees in the Sinai Desert—a prospect that would mean
the end of the Palestinian cause and denying the refugees
their inalienable right of return. Demonstrations spread all
over the Gaza Strip and were held for many days, as people
expressed their opposition to and their displeasure with the
Egyptian collusion with the plan. Life in Gaza was paralyzed
and the Egyptians could not control the situation, so they
jailed hundreds of people, including Mu'in. At that time,
there were many political prisoners in Egyptian prisons, so
Mu'in got to know many authors, writers, and intellectuals.
After the end of the war and the Israeli withdrawal, I became

part of a group of students who received permission from the prison administration to visit and help some political prisoners; so we took fruit, money, cigarettes, and shirts as presents and visited them. Mu'in asked me what I was going to do after I finished university, and I said I wanted to teach in Gaza schools to help my people, especially refugees, and I did so. Later, Mu'in would tell me how my words and determination captured his heart and mind.

In 1957, after the Israeli withdrawal and return of the Egyptian administration, I returned to Gaza and lived with my grandparents, aunts, and cousins. There were celebrations everywhere in the Gaza Strip, and tens of thousands of people danced in the streets, crying from happiness and celebrating the withdrawal of the Israelis and the end of the occupation. They danced and sang on Omar Al Mukhtar Street until two in the morning to welcome the return of the Egyptian administrative governor. I wish I could now celebrate the withdrawal of the Israeli occupation as we did then.

My ambition was to teach the refugee students in any of Gaza's refugee camps, but I wasn't allowed to work in the UNRWA schools as the priority was to hire refugees, not Indigenous Gazans. Instead, from 1957 to 1959, I taught social science, philosophy, and psychology at Al Zahra Secondary School, where my aunt, Yusra, was headmistress. Many people visited the school because it was very clean, very disciplined, and had many activities. There were sports and social and political activities, and every week we invited community leaders and other important people in Gaza and from different professions to talk about many topics. We supervised many groups in the school, and the students put together school newspapers and magazines in which they

*Sahbaa (centre, in the light-coloured shirt) with her high school
students in Gaza, preparing for a school exhibition, 1950s.*
(Photo courtesy of Sahbaa's family)

wrote about whatever they wanted. In 1958, sixty students
along with the headmistress and some teachers from the
school went to Cairo to participate in a conference on Afro-
Asian Solidarity for Palestinians. At that time, the Palestinian
issue had been put on ice, and although many delegations
came to visit the refugee camps, I felt that these were like
visits to an exhibition or museum and not to help or promote
the issue of Palestinian refugees.

I received my Bachelor of Arts in January 1958, four
months after I started work. I was allowed to work before I
graduated because teachers were needed, and I had passed
all the exams except French. My classes were in Arabic and
English, but we had a compulsory French class because
Egyptians study two foreign languages. But during my four

years of study, I didn't care for French and didn't study it, so I had to take French classes before I received my certificate. I sat for the exam in Cairo, passed it, and graduated.

The time I spent as a teacher in Gaza City was one of the greatest times of my life. I consider teaching to be one of the highest professions as it deals with human beings, helps in forming their characters, and shapes future generations. It was a difficult time, and many students suffered from various kinds of problems; the anguish could be easily spotted on their faces. I believe the teacher's role is to try to engage with students and help them manage their problems, ease their discomfort, and provide them with information, strategies, tools, knowledge, and morals like honesty and truth, in order to prepare them to deal with life—or at least try. This is all in addition to teaching them to read and write and be a healthy member of society.

After the Israeli army withdrew from Gaza in 1957, my brother, who was friends with Mu'in, visited my aunts and me because Mu'in had told him that he wanted to marry me. I was very surprised because I had only met him a few times, and the first was in jail. I was also hesitant and afraid because I had heard and read many stories about poets, especially about their imagination and sensitivity, because of which they were temperamental and needed understanding and patience. I wondered about my ability to live with such a personality. It was a hard and scary idea even to think about becoming engaged to a poet. At the time, Mui'n was a teacher at an UNRWA school at the Jabalya refugee camp, located north of Gaza City. He worked there despite the fact that he wasn't a refugee; but in 1952, there were many schools and few qualified teachers among the refugees. Later, when refugees became more qualified, the UNRWA schools made it a priority to hire them because Gazans had their own schools, land, and work. Mu'in visited our school regularly with his friends and came to meet my aunt, Yusra, who was the headmistress of the school then, to discuss issues related to education. We had no contact with him in the communist party, although he was a big leader and a well-known poet. He had a very good reputation in Gaza, so I told my brother I would think about it. After careful thinking and getting some advice from friends and family members, I agreed, so my brother accepted Mu'in's proposal of marriage on my behalf. But my mother, who was still in Cairo, then asked him to come and see her to ask for my hand, because she knew that Mu'in was a communist and had been in prison.

After Mu'in was released from prison in 1957, he was prevented from travelling outside of Gaza without permission from Egyptian intelligence because he was a known communist and political activist, so he asked Dr. Haidar Abd Al Shafi to speak to the Egyptian administration in Gaza for him. Dr. Abd Al Shafi was a good friend of Mu'in and our family. He was a well-known national figure and respected community leader who had started the Palestine Red Crescent Society. He was also a respected man and listened to by the Egyptians. So, Mu'in was escorted by a soldier and allowed to go to Cairo for two days to meet my mother.

During the 1950s, there had been great support for the Marxist ideology among the people of Iraq, and to some extent in Egypt, Syria, Lebanon, and Jordan. It was popular in those Arab countries and had tens of thousands of supporters. There was also a communist party in Gaza, but it was secret and had ties with the party in Egypt, which was small but very active. The Arab governments, including

Abd Al Nasser, saw the Marxists as a threat to their power. So, Abd Al Nasser along with King Hussein arrested all the communist members and anyone suspected of being one or of having a communist tie. They were subjected to harsh repression from both the Jordanian Kingdom and the Egyptian government.[12] In January 1957, King Hussein removed the parliamentary immunities of parliament's elected members that had made them immune from prosecution, sentencing them to imprisonment.[13] Similarly, communists were crushed in Egypt. The party became illegal and the campaign against them reached Gaza.[14] Protests were organized by the Egyptian administration to support Abd Al Nasser's policies. So, people and students demonstrated against me at my school, and against other comrades at other schools. But the biggest protest was against Mu'in at his school. Palestinian students shouted that they didn't want communists—unbelievers of God and infidels—in the school, and the Egyptians, who supervised the schools together with the Egyptian police, watched the demonstrations on the sidelines of what they had orchestrated and inspired. The students were young and carried signs with slogans, shouting against communists in the playground before they headed to their classes. They were encouraged by their teachers, many of them Egyptians, who told them what they should say (and even prepared the signs for them). In the mosques, the Muslim Brotherhood also demonstrated against the communists and nationalist movements, but after the communists were all arrested, they were afraid that they would be arrested as well. Nobody could speak.

3 / Arrest and Imprisonment

MU'IN AND I WERE ARRESTED during that campaign.
I was imprisoned for sixteen months and then released, and
Mu'in was imprisoned until March 1963.[1] I was at my grandfather's house when the head of intelligence services and two
other people knocked at the door at 1:00 A.M. looking for me.
I knew...and I had guessed that they would come. I was taken
to a hall where there were many people. After a short time,
we were all taken on a bus to Cairo that same night. They
also had arrested Mu'in, and when I left my grandfather's
house, I saw an ambulance at his aunt's house, where he was
living at the time. She told them that if they took him they
would take her heart, and that same night she died. I was the
only woman to be arrested along with ninety-six men.
Recently, when I visited my Aunt Yusra, she told me that
after I had left that night, the head of intelligence services
returned to my grandfather's home and stayed for two hours
apologizing to my grandmother and my aunt for arresting
me. He told them he was very sorry, but he had to obey the
orders. But he was very embarrassed because at that time
girls and women were never arrested, and he considered it
shameful to do such a thing. My aunt sent a bag of clothes

and necessities with the men when they left, which was very helpful for me.

I was accused of provocation and of the mobilization of students, and of trying to create their awareness of political issues and the causes of our suffering. Yes, I tried to raise awareness among my students, and I encouraged them to be open-minded and to learn about what was going on in the world. I taught them about the atomic bombs that had exploded in Hiroshima and Nagasaki. I explained to them the meaning of imperialism and exploitation, and about the Americans' attempts to be the only hegemony in the region. I encouraged them to read about the many revolutions and movements in the world to learn how to be intellectual, and I encouraged them to read other books besides studying the books of the curriculum. I took them to the school library and to the bookshops; I tried to inspire them to read and to analyze and research, and I took them on school trips so they could see the beauty of nature and the beauty of Gaza. This was not normally allowed in schools because teachers had to teach the curriculum and nothing else. But I never taught my students anything about Marxism or recruited them to that party or way of thinking. I just wanted to give them the opportunity to have experiences and to benefit from learning in the way most natural to them: through curiosity and exploration.

I had many books dealing with Marxism, but they were for myself to read and to learn from, and not for my students. I was always inspired by and gained hope and strength from history books that dealt with national liberation—and by how weak countries defeated colonization and became independent. My inner strength came from the worldwide international struggle against colonialism, and the power of those who have always fought for their freedom everywhere. For me, Che Guevara symbolized all the honest, resilient, and brave freedom fighters whose main goals were to combat oppression and to help the oppressed to achieve their freedom, rights, and dignity. What he symbolized and aspired to bothered the colonizers, and this is why he was killed. I am proud to say that I was one of the first women who knew about and studied Marxist ideology in Gaza, at a time when it was considered against our traditions, religion, and society.

In the prison, I wasn't interrogated or investigated, not even with one question, but was left there stranded without knowing a thing. The head of the prison asked me my name and why I was there, and I told him that he should raise those questions with the people who had brought me there. I was put in a room with a bed beside the administration room because I couldn't be imprisoned with the other prisoners, who were all male. They didn't torture me, but it was psychological torture because I could hear it happening to male prisoners in the room beside mine. Then a guard came and told me that when he entered the room I had to stand up, but I refused and told him that he should stand, not me. He asked why I was there, and I gave him the same answer I had given to the head of the prison, and he ordered one of the soldiers to take the bed outside of the room. I told him I didn't care, that I could sleep on the floor as it is healthier. In fact, many times I pretended to be very strong just to convince them that I was strong. But deep in my heart I was afraid and worried.

I told the guard, "I didn't commit any crime; I am here because I am a political prisoner and I have three rights. First, to be allowed to go to the toilet. Second, to keep the

light on, day and night. Third, to have some books, newspapers, or cultural material."

He sneered and said, "Do you have other orders for me?
And you also want to read newspapers in prison?"

"Why not? Why should I be isolated from what's going on
in the world?" I answered.

I was confined to this room for forty-two days, and
the only person I saw during this time was the guard who
brought my food and then left. But I was allowed to go to the
toilet and wash my clothes, and after a long fight my clothes
were ironed for me. I slept on a mattress on the floor, and
I used the bag that my aunt had sent for my pillow. During
that time, I didn't see the sun and didn't speak to anyone,
although sometimes I spoke to myself just to use and hear
my voice. For the first six days, I didn't eat anything because
the beans and bread I was given were full of weevils, the tea
was always cold, and the cup was chipped. When the doctor
came to see me, he saw that I had lost a lot of weight and
asked why my face was full of pimples, and I told him that
perhaps it was from constipation. He asked me why I didn't
eat and said that I should eat to stay alive. So, I started to
eat because I didn't know how long I would be in prison. At
the end of the forty-two days, I spent another four months
at that prison, but I was now allowed visitors. At first, when
my mother and sister came to visit, I couldn't speak to them
because I wasn't able to use my voice from not talking during
my isolation. They were astonished at my ironed clothes and
I told them that now the guards were good to me. My mother
brought me things every week, and I was allowed to leave the
room for an hour every afternoon to walk in the yard. Before
I left the prison, the Egyptian officer told my mother that
they respected me because I knew my rights.

Then I was moved to another jail, where I joined other Egyptian political prisoners who were arrested during that time. There, we weren't allowed visitors, and some Egyptian prisoners hadn't been visited for years. I remember one prisoner who had a baby in the prison, and when she was released with him, he was five years old and hadn't ever seen a visitor. Every month, our families sent us toothpaste, soap, winter or summer clothes, and sheets through the administration, but they were searched very thoroughly before being given to us. We celebrated birthdays, wedding anniversaries, birthdays of the prisoners' children, and national occasions. We learned embroidery, sewing, and knitting, and made things like jackets, embroidered tablecloths, and pullovers for the prisoners' children. Work like cleaning and tidying the beds inside our section was divided among us. We also listened to the news and sometimes read newspapers and magazines. Actually, these things were forbidden, but the long-term offenders shared them with us because they respected the political prisoners. During prison searches, they took and hid the radios, newspapers, and other things for us so that we would not be questioned by the prison administration.

Prison was a very good experience for me. I learned so much. There were twenty really intellectual and intelligent women, among them journalists, teachers, and artists, and one had a master's degree. They were all members of the communist party. One taught us French, and one taught us how to speak English with a good accent. We read Arabic stories and newspapers and discussed the situation in Cuba in the aftermath of the success of Fidel Castro's revolution, when they managed to overthrow the Batista dictatorship back in early 1959. I was so much younger than them so they could better discuss, critique, and analyze the situation in Egypt, which was different to that of Palestine and the rest of the world. Together, we studied and discussed many movements and matters that were going on in the world. The people who arrested the political prisoners were foolish because when people are put together in a small, confined place there is freedom to talk. So, we collaborated with one another; we shared knowledge and experiences, and discussed all sorts of topics and issues. We could comfortably say anything without any sort of censorship and give any opinion, and we always discussed everything. I also learned how to be organized, to be tidy, to listen to others, to respect others, to follow the rules, and even how to bring prohibited things into the prison and hide them—like papers, pens, newspapers, and radios. I learned so much, and the benefits were enormous. I still remember them and their names with great appreciation. One became a well-known painter, another became a famous artist in Egyptian theatre and cinema, and one still sends her good wishes to me even today.

A year after I arrived, a woman prison officer told me I was to be released the next day. Usually, prisoners were told one day before, so they could prepare to leave. When the other prisoners heard, they organized a big celebration for me that lasted the whole night, so we didn't sleep. The next morning I was ready and gave everything I didn't need to the prisoners. A Palestinian officer working with the Egyptians escorted me from the prison to a hotel in Cairo to wait for the train to Gaza. We stayed a night in the hotel, and he phoned my family to come to the hotel to see me before I returned to Gaza. It was so nice, because it had been a long time since I had seen them. Early the next morning we took

the train to Gaza and arrived late, so I spent that night at
Al Saraya, which had become the centre for the Egyptian
administration after the British left Gaza. I contacted my
family early the next morning to come and sign me out of
the prison, and within an hour my relative came and signed
the formal papers, and I was free.

After my release, I found out I was fired from my work,
and my travel documents were seized from me for the
year that followed as a form of punishment. I was free
from prison, but I was forbidden to teach or travel outside
of Gaza. Finally, and after several attempts, the Egyptian
administration allowed me to work in the education office,
where I was an administrator and typist who did the
budgets, typed letters, and sometimes made schedules for
the teachers. In those times, I prepared many things for my
future house, read many, many books, and learned some
English so as to develop my skills.

I secretly went to some local and well-respected doctors
including Dr. Haidar Abd Al Shafi, who I thought might be
sympathetic, to ask for help in sending assistance to some
political prisoners (among them Mu'in, because neither his
family nor I could visit him). I didn't want the Egyptians to
know I was still active because I felt that I was still under
observation. Although it was a humanitarian gesture, at the
time everything was mixed up, and I didn't want to seem
conspicuous. These doctors and the families of the prisoners
asked the Egyptian administration if they could send care
packages with basic first aid provisions, medicine, cigarettes,
and toothpaste, and the prisoners were then allowed to have
these packages every month.

In 1963, Abd Al Nasser began to realize the role of the
communists and other political and grassroots groups, and

that without these movements he couldn't work. He also began to realize the value of having community and political leaders to build the society to empower him and Egypt, especially when he faced the difficulty of financing the Aswan High Dam, which he constructed after the British left to prevent the Nile from flooding. This project required a lot of money, but the World Bank had too many conditions for the loan, so he nationalized the Suez Canal and took the income and built the high dam with the help of the Soviet Union. After he died, some people said the high dam killed the fish and weakened the land, but after the Sudan flooded, they thanked God that the dam had saved them from the floods.

The West felt threatened by Abd Al Nasser, his ideas, and his discourses, as well as his support for the decolonization movements in the Arab world. He was trying to unite the Arab nations, but it was not in the interests of the imperialists to have a developed, united, and strong Arab leadership. The West wanted a market for their goods, and the Arab world to be dependent on them. Egypt was also receiving good weapons and military aid from the Soviet Union, which would balance the power between the Arabs and Israel, but the West wanted the balance of power to always tilt toward Israel. Abd Al Nasser also believed that anything taken by force could only be returned by force. And this applied to Israel, which occupied Arab land. At that time, there were many advisers from China and the Soviet Union who supplied Egypt with good weapons, and this was threatening for the West and its interests in the region.

Abd Al Nasser expected a war, so he gathered educated people and nationalists and popular leaders around him and released the political prisoners to benefit from their experiences. He gave them important positions in the ministries, because the political situation made it necessary for the powers to be united in order to work for the benefit of the country. So, he issued resolutions that allowed nationalist and political movements and parties, including the communists, to be active. To strengthen the economy, he adopted Arab socialism as the official ideology of the state. This step encouraged economic development, supported the peasants and farmers, and nationalized many projects, banks, and enterprises.

51

4 / Marriage and Exile

MU'IN WAS RELEASED with the other political prisoners in March 1963. I knew he would be released when I read in a newspaper that a group of prisoners might be discharged on a certain date. They were also the last group in the prison to be released; others who were caught at the same time had been released earlier. When he was released, I went with my Aunt Yusra to see him at his aunt's house. We then began preparations for our wedding.

In July 1963, after I had waited five years for him, I married Mu'in in Gaza. My family and our friends, neighbours, and teachers attended the wedding, and Mu'in's family came from Lebanon. My mother, who had returned to live in Gaza, and Mu'in's mother made the arrangements for a small ceremony. My sister in Egypt sewed the wedding dress and veil and sent it to me across the border. On our wedding day, my younger sister prepped me and applied my makeup. The party was held on the roof of Mu'in's family home, and I remember we went in a car around Gaza with the horn blaring in celebration to show that we were finally married. Mu'in and I prepared his family home, where we lived until 1966 before moving to Lebanon. Our furniture was bought from the Council of

Sahbaa and Mu'in Bseiso at their wedding, Gaza, 1963.
(Photo courtesy of Sahbaa's family)

Churches, but we lost it all during shipping. It never arrived
and we don't know where it went.

I married Mu'in Bseiso, the educator, the activist,
the author, the freedom fighter, and most importantly, the
Palestinian national poet. I lived with him for twenty-two
years. Now, poets have different lives than others. They are
sometimes unusual in their ways of thinking or how they see
the world. Being a poet and intellectual meant he needed
to read a lot, especially translated materials and books, and
reviews of international and Arabic poetry, and he needed a
decent environment to help him be creative. He also needed
someone who could understand him and think long term.
And I did all that I could to support him and his work. I

did so because I believed in Mu'in, and in his role and his
national mission as a talented writer to create strong, brave,
and sharp words that would highlight our national struggle
and encourage our people to continue their struggle toward
freedom. I loved Mu'in and I believed in him. This is why I
suspended most of my activities and allocated the bulk of my
time to providing him with the best environment to write.
I believed that he had a national obligation and duty before
him, and I had to help because his words would speak for
Palestine and for Palestinians and would mobilize and help
the next generation in building the future of our nation.

Mu'in was a poet who used words as weapons to
strengthen the people's spirits and inspire and rally them.
He produced the most beautiful poems and literature and
had very strong political opinions regarding the events of
the time. Before I married him, he had only written three
poems: *The Battle* in 1952; *Egyptian Poems*, with the cooperation of some Egyptian poets; and *The Giant Ears of Wheat*,
about his experiences in the 1956 war. But after we were
married, he wrote many works, including plays, poems,
articles, books, and even children's stories. His poems were
translated into many languages. He became a member of
the Palestinian Writers' Union and the Afro-Asian Writers'
Union, and he later became the vice editor-in-chief of the
latter's magazine, *The Lotus*, in 1979. He contributed to a
magazine in Cairo, for which he became editor. After the
signing of the Camp David Accords of 1979, the magazine
was transferred to Beirut and he became its editor. However,
after the 1982 Israeli invasion of Lebanon, the magazine
was moved again, to Tunis this time. He participated in
conferences and meetings, and I was always understanding
and never complained about his absences. I loved and

understood Mu'in and appreciated his efforts and his work. I enjoyed his work, his breaks, his thoughts, his discussions with me, his laugh, and his extraordinary energy, and especially his love of Palestine and of Gaza. We were a happy couple and I miss him all the time. It is an honour to have been the wife of the poet Mu'in Bseiso. Hopefully the time will come when a big association will publish his collective works and his legacy will become known by the present and future generations. This admiration is not only because he was my husband, but because of the pure dedication, love, and passion he had for both our cause and our people.

Mu'in worked as a teacher at Khuza'a School in Khan Younis for a year after we were married, and in September 1964 he was appointed headmaster at Salah Al Deen School in Gaza City. I continued my work as a secretary until October 1966. We had three children: two daughters and a son. My first child was Dalia, and although I had no problems during my pregnancy, after the delivery I bled severely. Movement in Gaza at that time was restricted during the night—not exactly curfews, but similar—and the doctor couldn't come on his own, so we had to call an ambulance for him to be able to examine me. I suffered a lot during that delivery, and it was good that my mother was with me in Gaza to take care of the baby and me. She taught me how to look after Dalia because she was the first. Life was very difficult at that time and hard for working women who had many responsibilities with work, children, and a husband. There were no child-minding centres, so I left Dalia with my aunt, but when my son Tawfiq came, it became too much for her, so I found a lady to look after them. I gave her 10 Egyptian pounds from my salary of 39 pounds; this meant a quarter of my salary was being allocated for childcare.

We lived outside of Palestine for thirty years: eleven years in Beirut, over a year in Damascus, eight months in Libya, three years in Egypt, and fourteen years in Tunis. Mu'in left Gaza early in 1966 and went to Beirut, Lebanon, where his family lived, and we followed in October. He wanted to be better connected to the Arabic and international literature there, as Beirut at that time was, and still is, a centre for international culture and a hub for creative intellectuals. I often felt remorse because I had left Gaza, but the situation at that time was stronger than our wishes. Mu'in needed the freedom to think and write, and we didn't think for a moment that Gaza would be occupied with the rest of Palestine. We never imagined that the 1967 defeat would happen, and that we would become refugees and not be able to return to our land.

He didn't find work in Beirut, so he went to Kuwait for a short time. After I joined him, he left us again, this time to go back to Beirut. In Kuwait, he participated in poets' meetings and wrote plays for Kuwaiti radio to support the Palestinian cause. He also organized meetings for poets, writers, and journalists to advocate for Palestine, and organized demonstrations that called upon the government to support the Palestinians.

At that time, Mu'in's family were living in Beirut again, after they had left Gaza and gone to work in Kuwait for a while. When Mu'in was arrested in 1959, they had come from Kuwait to visit him. They had planned to stay in Gaza, but they were prevented from returning permanently by the Egyptians because of Mu'in's political activities and the volatile situation in general, so they went to Lebanon and settled there. So, when we moved to Beirut, we lived with his family for five months because Mu'in didn't have any income and was looking for work.

We travelled to Syria in April 1967. Mu'in had many friends there and he found work at a newspaper, writing articles and a column. When the 1967 war began, we moved to my sister's house, where I looked after the children because she was a doctor and spent most of her time at the hospital. Her husband was called up to serve at the front, Mu'in was at the newspaper, and I was alone at home with my sister's son and my two children, so I read everything about the situation and listened to the news all the time. The war was unexpected, and it was a very strong defeat. It was like the end of hope. And of course we smelled the involvement of conspiracy and treason in the event as it was happening. There were many questions about the fall of the Syrian Golan Heights, the fall of the Egyptian Sinai Peninsula, the number of victims, and the ugly defeat. As a result, we were all so frustrated, sad, and broken. My sister would return home for short periods and tell me about the dead and wounded soldiers, the victims and their tragic stories, the terrible situation, and the shock of the defeat. It was a really tough time for my sister, dealing with all of this horror, and a tough time for all of us trying to comprehend the shocking news and later the utter defeat.

Mu'in returned home early every morning with the newspaper and a Kalashnikov rifle, which he was given as protection in case the newspaper was attacked. In fact, he didn't know how to use a weapon at all, but it was an emergency situation; so, like others, he was given this weapon to help if necessary or in case we were attacked. After the war, we left my sister's home and rented a flat, as Mu'in had regular work and an income.

Israel initiated the 1967 war to defeat Abd Al Nasser, and
after this defeat Abd Al Nasser initiated the war of attrition
against Israel—there was a lot of military training, which
lifted the Egyptian army's morale. Abd Al Nasser built his
army and provided it with good weapons with help from the
Soviet Union, and the result was that they achieved a great
victory in 1973 in which they broke through the Bar Lev
Line.[1] This was the outcome of a well-planned strategy and
tactics. The Arab world felt much better as they had restored
part of their dignity with the 1973 victory and because they
had liberated part of their land. They had also defeated the
Israeli army, which had been described and deemed as the
invincible force. This proved that if you have a strong will
and strategy you can win. All of these good efforts together
contributed to that victory, and this is what Sadat harvested
in 1973.

It wasn't the victory we dreamed of, though, because we
still believed that if the Egyptians had continued the war,
they could have achieved many things and returned the
Sinai, while also liberating the Gaza Strip. I believe that if
this had been the case, then many of the Palestinian rights
could have been returned without much compromise.
But the war stopped according to an outside order, which
conspired against the continuance of the Arab victory and
eventually led to the first Camp David and the signing of the
first peace treaty with Israel. The Palestinian cause became
isolated, especially after Egypt was taken out of this conflict.

After the 1967 defeat, the political situation was very
difficult, and we left Syria in 1968 because of problems with
Mu'in's work at the newspaper. He had written an article
that was critical of its policy and was demoted from his position as one of its main editors. He was then invited by the

Afro-Asian Writers' Union to a conference in Moscow. We didn't have money to pay the rent for the house, and Mu'in wasn't sure that he would return to Syria because he didn't like the work, so we left. Oil had recently been discovered in Libya and my brother, the engineer, was working there for a French oil exploration company, so I took the children to his home because my mother and sisters were there. Libya had been under the rule of the Italians, so many products such as shoes, furniture, and food were Italian. The buildings were new and very clean, with compounds near the beach. There was a very big American oil company called Al Huwalis. Many educated Palestinians lived in Libya, and a group of Palestinians from Jaffa had a lot of land that was planted with olive and citrus trees. When anyone visited this land, it felt like a piece of Jaffa. Once we travelled from Tripoli to Cairo by car; then we went to Ben Ghazi, about 2,000 kilometres away, where we stayed a week or two with my uncle, who was working as a doctor there, and then drove the same distance back again to Cairo.

I stayed in Libya for about eight months. During this time Mu'in translated his first book, *Palestine Poems*, in Moscow, where two hundred thousand copies were distributed. We then moved to Cairo and lived in my mother's home from 1969 to 1972, as she was still in Libya. I registered the children at a private school. Mu'in found work at one of the most popular newspapers in Egypt, and he collected all his printed newspaper articles into a book, *The Literature of Jumping with Parachutes*, which was published in Cairo. New poets, writers, and friends gathered at our home, and I also re-established contact with old friends from the neighbourhood and my university days. We stayed in Cairo for three years and started to settle, but I had a feeling that we would leave again. Mu'in always told me that we must always be ready to leave because exile is not, and cannot be, an alternative for the homeland. We didn't feel stable in Cairo because we were living in my mother's house and not in our own home, and as we were living in another Arab country, but not our homeland. In addition, we were ready to leave at any minute, especially if Mu'in wrote an article that might be considered critical of the general policy of Egypt or the newspaper. This would become the case in 1970 after Abd Al Nasser's death, and during the era of President Sadat, who began to imprison Abd Al Nasser's followers and political activists. The situation was unstable and unpredictable. So, we once again returned to Beirut where we stayed until 1982, when the PLO was obliged to leave for Tunisia.[2]

Despite the long time we spent there, we didn't feel stable in Beirut either. Yes, Lebanon is a very beautiful country, but we were always threatened by Israeli war planes attacking Palestinians in the refugee camps and the assassinations of their leaders and activists. We were accompanied by assassinations and killings wherever we went. Three prominent Palestinian leaders—the writer and poet Kamal Nasser, Kamal Edwan, and Abu Yusuf Al Najjar—were assassinated in 1973 by an Israeli group led by Ehud Barak, who later became prime minster. A year earlier, in 1972, the famous Palestinian writer and journalist Ghassan Kanafani, together with his niece who happened to be with him in the car, were assassinated by a Mossad bomb planted in his automobile.[3] When the Mossad assassinated Kanafani, I became very worried about Mu'in.

The cycle of assassinations continued. In Cyprus, Hanna Muqbil, another Palestinian writer, was assassinated, and then Al Hamshari in Paris,[4] and Majed Abu Sharar in Rome, and many others. So I really became worried, especially being in Beirut during the Lebanese war. But it is the case that whoever works in politics and activism is always on high alert. It doesn't mean that one should stop the fight for freedom or the fight for rights and dignity; on the contrary, life has to continue, as there is no other alternative but to keep going and to have optimism, faith, and hope. In assassinating poets and writers, Israel assassinated the pen, the word, and art. And in killing the Palestinian leaders and activists, Israel assassinated humanity. This policy is still going on unabated and unchallenged. The Israeli army is carrying out the same policies of assassination and targeting our political leaders and civil society figures in the present *Intifada*, and no one in the Western governments seems to care.[5]

In 1972, Tawfiq and Dalia were now in elementary school and Malika was six months old. When she was four years old, she went to the French school in Beirut. It was the first time that we really lived with the Lebanese. Mu'in mainly worked at home, where he recited his poems while I typed for him. I typed up *Palestinian Notebooks*, and in 1978 he published his complete works in one book. I stayed most of the time in Beirut, so I didn't see much of Lebanon. The only way out of Beirut that I knew was the road that led to Damascus because I used to visit my sister, and from time to time, I travelled to Cairo with my children for a week or ten days to visit my family.

Then the clashes, wars, and siege against Palestinians started. We lived through all of them from 1972 to 1982. It was a very difficult time during the 1982 siege of Beirut. There was a severe shortage of food, with no bread, water, fruit, or vegetables, and people starved. We were not able

Sahbaa's children: Dalia, Tawfiq, and Malika, Cairo, 1970s.
(Photo courtesy of Sahbaa's family)

to move anywhere else. We lived in fear of the sudden and indiscriminate shelling that was happening at all times, nonstop. The shelling reached every corner and affected both the Palestinians and Lebanese, who paid a very heavy price during these Israeli invasions and attacks.

In 1973, the clashes started in the refugee camps, and we witnessed how the Palestinian refugees suffered. But the real war between the Palestinians and Lebanese, known as the camps war, started in 1975 when the militias of the Phalange, a right-wing political party of Lebanese Maronite Christians, killed twenty-seven Palestinians on a bus.[6] The situation for Palestinian refugees in Lebanon is different and much more difficult than in other Arab countries. In Egypt, Syria, and Jordan, the situation for Palestinians is much better.

They can own property, shops, factories, and businesses, and can study or work in any profession, but not in Lebanon. There, they are treated as third class citizens, deprived from working in over fifty-one professions. They have suffered great problems in Lebanon. To protect themselves and the refugees in the other refugee camps from the attacks of the Phalange militia (who opposed the Palestinian presence in Lebanon), Palestinians formed military groups that carried weapons. Lebanon has many political groups and factions and didn't need another one, and this sparked the war in the refugee camps. When Palestinians became a recogniz-able power there, they were accused of wanting to establish a state for themselves within the Lebanese state. So, it was decided that they would lash out against the Palestinians because they were seen as a threat by other Lebanese groups, namely the Maronites, or Phalange Party, who later became a close ally of Israel.

Then in 1978 came the Litany invasion, when Israel invaded the south of Lebanon and occupied 40 kilometres of Lebanese land, declaring it a security zone to protect what they said were their borders. Mu'in organized and partici-pated in demonstrations and recited his poems about the need to continue our struggle and resistance against the Israeli military occupation. I was worried about him being a poet and a fighter with words, calling for freedom against all kinds of colonization, occupation, racism, and dictatorial regimes. Whenever the hand of Mossad reached out to kill someone, my worries increased. Mu'in himself wrote about the danger he faced being a Palestinian poet and activist. In one of his articles he wrote, "when you want to write you have to learn how to swim in ink. For me, swimming in the ink is more dangerous to the poet than swimming at the sea.

You must be honest with yourself and with others. The poet is like mountain climbing; one goes up and down, and he must continue to climb until he reaches the summit."[7]

Then Israel invaded Lebanon in June 1982. Their policy is always the same, especially their assassination style: at Al Beqa' in Lebanon, they assassinated Sa'd Sayil, who was one of the greatest Palestinian leaders.[8] They assassinated Abu Touq, another brave and fearless Palestinian hero. He fought with a small group of Palestinian fighters against a strong assault from tanks when the Israelis wanted to occupy Sour. After the Israeli army had killed all the fighters, one of their officers said he didn't realize he was fighting children, because he saw they were all very young. Then in the battle of Shaqif Castle (also known as Belfort Castle, a very high and strong Crusader castle in southern Lebanon), the Israeli soldiers threw gas cylinders inside to kill everyone.[9] If they had not done so, they would have never been able to defeat those brave *Fedayeen*.

When Israel invaded Lebanon in 1982, Mu'in was in Kuwait to bury the body of his brother. He quickly returned via Syria and reached Beirut to be part of the struggle. The Palestinian refugee camps were far from the place where we lived, so I didn't know the situation exactly, only that Palestinians were prevented from entering eastern Beirut. It was possible for us to leave, but Mu'in insisted that we stay, remain steadfast in our struggle, and support our *Fedayeen*, who were fighting for our freedom and our rights. At this time, he wrote his very famous book *88 Days Behind the Barricades* (*Thamaniya wa thamanoun yowman khalf al mata-rees*), which he wrote by candlelight.[10] In that book, he told the stories of the siege of Beirut and the legendary resistance of Palestinians and the Lebanese to the Israeli aggression and brutality. There was no electricity or water, but he needed to write, so one after the other the candles would melt on his hands while he wrote. Despite any circumstance, he wanted the poetry to speak the truth, especially during the days of the Beirut siege. He worked day and night and used many candles, and when he ran out, he used the beautifully decorated ones he had brought from his trips abroad when he attended conferences. We were living on the fourth floor of a building, and if there was water, it didn't reach us. We were bombed from the air and our street was struck by shells, so we went to my mother-in-law's home. When her street was shelled, we were forced to find another place, then another place, and so we escaped from area to area, house to house, shelter to shelter, while the bombs left no place free from their turmoil. Lebanon was shelled and bombed every day and we expected death at any moment, but, thank God, we survived. We had also survived the year before, in 1981, when Israel bombed the PLO headquarters in West Beirut, killing hundreds of civilians.[11] I was there meeting a friend and had just left an hour before the attack occurred. Many times during the Israeli invasion, I thought of how I would die—whether it would be alone, or with people in a shelter, or with Mu'in, or in the street—because the shelling was destruction without jurisdiction and targeted anything Palestinian or Lebanese. It was a continuation of the Zionist ethnic cleansing project that started in 1948, which had aimed to eliminate the Palestinians, their culture, their history, and their production—simply put, anything related to Palestinians. It's the ultimate racism that Zionism is built on.

Mu'in contributed to a daily newsletter called *Al Ma'raka* (The Battle), which was published jointly by the Palestinian Union of Writers and the Lebanese National Movement. It was written to encourage the fighters and raise the morale of the people, and it was distributed for free during the siege of Beirut in 1982. Many Egyptian, Iraqi, Palestinian, and Lebanese writers living in Lebanon contributed, including Mahmoud Darwish, Samih Al Qasim, Ziad 'Abd Al Fattah, and Mu'in, and there were also cartoons by Naji Al 'Ali. The newspaper team gathered and compiled the newsletter in an office and changed their location from time to time so they wouldn't be shelled by the Israelis.

We lived close to Mu'in's father's home. Once, I was with his parents after our street was shelled, while Mu'in and others stayed at our home to finalize the newsletter before it was printed. That same night, a bomb fell in the middle of our home, and luckily Mu'in had already left and joined us. God saved him in the Lebanon war, but he was fated to die in London.

Mu'in's mother, Huda Al Shawa, was very sick and had little access to medical care. Mu'in was very worried about his mother, so when the siege intensified, he asked a friend, Layla Sayigh, a Christian journalist, to take Huda and our daughters out of Beirut. Layla drove them to Damascus by car. From there they flew to Dubai to live with Suhair, Mu'in's sister, to escape the shelling. He wanted to send me with them, but I refused and insisted on staying with him and my people during the difficult time. Tawfiq was studying in London, and when the war started he wanted to return, but the road from the airport to the middle of west Beirut, where we lived, wasn't safe.

It was a rich time for Mu'in's literature. In addition to his poems, he also wrote a column in the PLO newspaper called *Falsatin Althawra* (Palestine: The Revolution). He wrote a lot in Lebanon and collated the articles he wrote and published them in a book. He was always busy at PLO meetings, where he was a cultural consultant for Chairman Arafat. We were fighting for the same cause as the Lebanese, who have a deep knowledge of the Palestinian people and their tragedy, and there were many demonstrations to support them. Many Palestinian cadres were trained in Lebanon, and the PLO centre was where Chairman Arafat met world leaders and representatives from international organizations. There was a solid cultural institution, and a very active and vigorous Palestinian research centre with a library of tens of thousands of books and a multilingual translation unit where many Hebrew and English books and articles were translated into Arabic. It was all destroyed and looted by Israel during the war.

Leaving Lebanon was very difficult because I left eleven years of memories there, happy and sad. Eleven years is not a short time. There we had a home, friends, schools for the children, stories, hopes, and memories. The first group of the PLO left Beirut on August 22, 1982. Mu'in and I, along with his brother and his cousin, left with the first group of Palestinian *Fedayeen*. This happened according to the agreement between the PLO, Lebanon, and Israel, mediated by Henry Kissinger and Philip Habib, who were applying their "shuttle diplomacy."[12] But Israel rarely respects agreements, and it followed the PLO to Tunis and continued its violations by attacking the PLO personnel, institutions, and offices: proof that Israel doesn't seek peace.[13] A few days after the PLO's withdrawal, the Israeli army advanced into Beirut in violation of the agreement. The UN condemned the incursions into Beirut, but Israel ignored them and later allowed the Phalangist militia to slaughter Palestinian civilians in the Sabra and Shatila refugee camps.

Sahbaa with her husband Mu'in Bseiso at the home of leading Egyptian poet Salah Jahin in the early 1970s. Left to right: Mu'in, (first name unknown) Khoury, Saiza Nabrawi, Widad Mitri, Sahbaa.
(Photo courtesy of Sahbaa's family)

We were the only four civilians to go with the *Fedayeen* because some of the PLO families were in Jordan and no other civilians wanted to leave Lebanon. But Mu'in and I decided to leave, and when we were asked whether we wanted to go with the first ship, we registered with the French observers in charge of the list. They thought we were militants because we wore uniforms and carried Kalashnikovs like the *Fedayeen*. At that critical point in time, it only felt right for me not to dress in ordinary clothes, especially as the only woman on board. I wanted to express and embody the sense of unity and patriotism I felt by putting on the PLO uniform. For the rest of my life, I will never forget the moment of our departure. Lebanese and Palestinians lined the streets from the city stadium to the harbour and said farewell to us in tears, throwing rice and rosewater and ululating and shooting their rifles. I will always remember that emotional sight. Despite what was said about the relationship between the Lebanese and Palestinians, we were sent off as heroes. This raised our spirits and gave us the will to start a new battle and continue our fight for our freedom, our dignity, and our land. It was a difficult moment, impossible to forget, and the feeling is still hidden in my heart. In fact, words cannot express that moment at all.

When we left Lebanon, we weren't able to take our belongings. People were only allowed one bag, and I tried to take as much as I could of Mu'in's articles, publications, and things he had handwritten, as well as literature and belongings. I was very sad because I couldn't carry a particular file containing many reviews about one of Mu'in's plays, which I had cut from newspapers and magazines from different countries and pasted in a book that documented the date of each source and the article that it had been pulled out of. Now I don't know whether it was stolen, burned, or eaten by mice. I took some books from our library, but I had to leave most of them. I only took a very small number of photographs, ones that I was afraid would fall into Israeli hands, because it could be dangerous for the people in them. Later, our building porter who witnessed it told me that after we had left, Israeli soldiers burst into the house and took a large photo of Mu'in, the Palestinian poet Mahmoud Darwish, and Yasser Arafat, which hung in the entrance to the house, and shot at it. This man was from the northern part of Palestine and had a twenty-two-year-old son who was killed during the

Lebanese civil war by a bomb while he was at the university. We still phone each other now.

I left many personal things that I had made during my childhood in Gaza, and all of my children's clothes, books, and toys; everything was left, and I couldn't return for them. I just took our travel documents and formal papers belonging to the family, so really the bag was mostly Mu'in's writings, and these were the things that remained for me after his death. I kept this legacy by taking the papers from Beirut—in fact, we first took them with us from Gaza—and then to Damascus, then to Beirut, and then to other cities and other places. I kept moving this increasing legacy from place to place to keep it, and you can see part of it now. Now my home is here, in Palestine, and here is where we are going to stay and nobody will move us. To this land we belong, and here we will try to make new memories and, if we can, move forward from the pain and problems of the past.

We left on a Greek ship that was guarded by the French Navy because we were frightened that Israel would sink the ship we took otherwise, and when it arrived in Cyprus, we were welcomed by Greeks and Palestinians. We were perfect examples of the diaspora when we left Lebanon: my son in one place, my daughters in another, while Mu'in travelled to another place, and I was going to another. In fact, we didn't know what to do or where we were going to settle, or if there would be another war in the place we were going that would force us to leave again. From Cyprus, Mu'in went to London, then Moscow, and then, after the PLO leadership arrived there, to Tunisia, where he rented a house.

5 / Tunis

WE LEFT BEIRUT ON AUGUST 22, 1982 and went to
Cairo. When we had settled in, my daughters came from
Dubai to join me, and we stayed until Malika finished her
school year. Dalia attended the British Council to study for
the TOEFL because the war had started in Lebanon before
she was able to sit for her TOEFL certificate, which she
needed to enter university.

I was in Cairo when I heard the news of the Sabra and
Shatilla massacres. Before the massacres took place, I had
felt a weird feeling that something terrible was going to
happen. The newly-elected Lebanese president, Bashir
Gemayel, was assassinated on September 14, 1982, and
everyone thought a Palestinian had killed him. But later
it was discovered that the assassin was Lebanese.[1] Before
Gemayel was assassinated, he had travelled to Israel to
meet with Prime Minister Menachem Begin. After the
meeting, he refused to comply with their orders to sign a
peace agreement with them.[2] Although many people were
happy that Gemayel, a close Maronite collaborator and
ally of Israel, was dead, I don't know why, but I felt something bad would happen. Two days later, on September 16,
the Sabra and Shatila massacres were committed. When

the Israelis entered West Beirut, they were received with
flowers and even dancing by the Phalange Maronite militia,
the well-known enemy of the Palestinians and the PLO. It
was before the internet, so we couldn't get the story and
pictures when the massacres happened—it was not like the
media today. But we knew how horrible they were, and that
a large number of victims were slaughtered just because
they were Palestinian. During the massacres, the Israeli
army surrounded the Palestinian camps to prevent the
refugees from leaving and facilitated the entry of the militiamen linked to the Phalange. The Israeli flares lit up the
camps' alley to facilitate the mission of the Phalange militia
who entered the camps and killed, raped, and disfigured
hundreds of Palestinian men, women, and children. The
massacres went on for three days and claimed the lives of
over three thousand Palestinian civilians. Sharon turned a
blind eye to what the Israeli proxy was doing. The news even
talked about him providing them with bulldozers to hide
their crimes.

A year after the massacres, in 1983, an Israeli court determined that Sharon bore the responsibility for the slaughter
of the refugees as the massacres took place under his army's
watch. Now this war criminal is the Prime Minister of Israel,
and he is continuing his crimes against us in full view of
the world that opts to turn a blind eye to the atrocities we
suffer. When I heard about the massacres, I became very
sick and depressed for a very long time. I could not eat for
several days, and when I saw the pictures in the papers and
on TV screens, I could not believe the horror. Despite being
a strong woman who hardly ever cries, I could not prevent
myself when I saw the reports and I sobbed in a hysterical
way. A few months after the massacres, the UN General

Assembly declared them an act of genocide.[3] This was not news for us, the Palestinians. We had witnessed this in the 1948 *Nakba*, then in the 1956 and 1967 wars, and we are witnessing it now in this *Intifada*—outright assaults on our people and our mere existence.

The beginning of our lives in Tunis was difficult. As in every new place, the start was difficult, with financial problems, work problems, settling in, and learning a new way of life in a new country that we didn't know. True, it is an Arab country and Arab society, but it was still different from ours, and from the Lebanese and Egyptian societies where I had lived. About four thousand families left Beirut. We knew each other and most were friends, and so we lived in Tunis as a Palestinian community. We visited other Palestinians and they visited us. I felt as though I was being pushed into a deeper exile, even further away from my homeland. I was exhausted and broken from being uprooted. The departure from Beirut was another potent reminder of our ceaseless cycle of displacement, let alone the deep sadness after the Sabra and Shatila massacres. It is a wound in the heart that I fear will never heal. So, I did not exert much effort to make Tunisian friends during those fourteen years.

The Tunisians helped Palestinians at a very critical time, but we also repaid their help. We helped the economy flourish as we did in Lebanon, and we didn't cause problems or destruction (as some accused us of in Lebanon). We went to their schools, rented their homes, bought their products, and paid utilities and telephone bills like everyone else. Tunis was also more expensive than Lebanon. Four thousand families, if not more, lived there in addition to PLO visitors and delegations, which required hotels and facilities. Wherever Palestinians go, they plant, build, and make life.

After the 1948 *Nakba*, many Palestinians, hundreds of thousands of them, teachers, engineers, doctors, nurses, and general labourers, went to the Arab Gulf countries and worked. In Kuwait alone, there have been about a quarter of a million Palestinians.

We lived in Tunis for four months, and then Mu'in went to London and it was his final stage in life. He died there on January 23, 1984, in a London hotel room, at a time when he was very exhausted, sick of the political situation, and still broken after what had happened in Sabra and Shatila. We were told that he had a severe heart attack and had been dead in his room for two days before anyone knew. He couldn't even ask for help from the hotel staff. We were also told that he had put a "Do Not Disturb" sign outside the door so they didn't bother him, but in my opinion, it was the hotel's obligation to check on him. How can a customer stay for two days without asking for a cup of coffee or using the telephone? At least they have to come every day to clean. I blame them, and I still believe that we should take them to court.

His death was the greatest loss of my life. The news was like a thunderbolt because, despite my fears through certain times, I hadn't expected it to happen. At the time, we were in exile and in great need of him, because the children were growing up and yearned for him to be beside them in their youthful years of starting their lives. They had become close in the last four months; in fact, they felt stable in his presence because he was mainly writing at home. Before, he had travelled a lot to participate in conferences and meetings, so he was like a presence and an absence at the same time. And sometimes he didn't speak to his children for days, just sat on the balcony, staring into space, and I knew he was reacting to or struggling with an idea, trying to create a poem. Losing him was very difficult because I had to be both mother and father, and I suffered a lot in piecing my life and the children's lives together. It wasn't an easy task at all.

Mu'in's body was brought from London to Tunis, but his family and I didn't want him buried there because it was too far to visit his grave, so we decided to bury him in Cairo. We couldn't even bury him in Gaza because the Israeli authorities refused to allow us to bring his body home. We searched for two days to find a place and then a man let us have a plot in a cemetery, which is now the martyrs' cemetery. He had a very big funeral in Cairo because he was well known, and many friends, writers, and Egyptian, Jordanian, Palestinian, and Arab intellectuals attended. After the funeral, I went alone to Tunis and began the lone battle of raising the children and helping them start their way in life. Dalia went to study business administration at Warnborough College at Oxford, and Malika continued her studies at the French school in Tunisia. When she finished her schooling, Malika attended the Ecole superieure de publicite in Paris, France, and studied advertising. Tawfiq suffered a lot after his father's death. It was a very difficult time for him because he couldn't accustom himself to the sudden loss and vacuum of Mu'in's presence. They had started to be friends and were becoming close. He stayed a long time in Tunis and didn't know what to do or how to overcome this crisis. He was devastated, to the point where he lost meaning in life and felt that life without his father wasn't a life at all. Finally, he found his way and attended the school of printing in Leipzig University, East Germany. At that time, it was one of the most renowned schools in East and West Germany.

The PLO helped a lot in assisting clever young refugees and exiled people to study, and all my children received scholarships from them. The communist states also helped in providing scholarships and seats for Palestinian students at their universities, where priority was given to the children of martyrs, PLO employees, prisoners, and political figures. After graduation, both of my daughters managed to find work. Malika worked in Dubai, and Dalia worked at the political office of the PLO and was in charge of the scholarships department.

Although Tunisia is a very beautiful country, we spent a very hard time there. The war on us in Lebanon that forced us to leave wasn't enough for the Israelis; they followed us to Tunis. Israel wanted to prove to Palestinians that it could reach anyone anywhere, including our leaders, even if it was at the ends of the earth. After the PLO left Lebanon, they rebuilt a headquarters in Tunisia, and within three years they were organized and back on their feet. By 1985, the PLO had resumed its previous activities, now from Tunis. In the same year, Israeli military planes attacked the Hammam Chott area, which was considered the PLO base.[4] The assault was planned to kill Yasser Arafat and the top leadership of the PLO. Luckily, Arafat was not at the base at the time of the attack, in which over sixty Palestinians were killed and many others injured, including Tunisians. Now there is a cemetery there in Hammam Chott with the names of all the martyrs from that attack.[5]

After 1982, the Palestinian issue was highlighted internationally, and the relationship between the leadership in the diaspora and occupied Palestine was strengthened when the first *Intifada* erupted in 1987. We demonstrated to the world that Palestinians are like a phoenix rising from the ashes, and it brought us back to life, especially the Palestinians of the diaspora. The *Intifada* returned our dignity and pride, and our belief in ourselves. We identified with the *Intifada* in Tunis, and extensive literature was issued by the PLO about the activists and activities, including magazines, pamphlets, and articles. Many festivals were held in support of the *Intifada*, and I should mention the Carthage festival where Marcel Khalifa, a famous Lebanese singer, sang for Palestine and the *Intifada*. Tens of thousands of people attended, and those who couldn't find seats climbed the light poles to see and hear him perform. Tunisians and other Arabs were sympathetic to the Palestinian cause and they supported the justice of our struggle.

| In Tunis, we also lost Mu'in's father, and I was very sad when he died. He was an open-minded and sensitive man, who had studied at Al Frireh School in Jaffa at the beginning of the twentieth century and knew the German, French, and Turkish languages. You can't imagine how the *Nakba* and the *Shatat* (exile and the suffering of dispersion) affected him. He was so afraid of dying outside of Palestine, but this is what happened. He died in 1988, and until the last days of his life he retained the hope of returning to his home, especially during the first *Intifada*, which had such a strong impact and had given hope to Palestinians all over the world. My father-in-law followed the news every hour and read everything in the newspapers related to the *Intifada*. He died in the diaspora, broken-hearted and dispossessed. It was sad for him to lose two of his sons during his life, and all these tragedies and problems affected him very much. He left this world without knowing the fate of his children or his nation. At the same time, the husband of Mu'in's only sister, Suhair, also died, and the loss added to our mourning. Death and fate fragmented us. Suhair took her mother and sons to Cairo

after she lost her husband, and I felt empty. She had worked in the Arab League in Tunis when it moved there from Cairo after the signing of the Camp David Accords (1978). Then the Arab League returned to Cairo, and when she moved, she went back to work there. Being in Tunis at that time was also difficult because it meant being far from your country at a vulnerable time when you felt it needed you most.

Every year, Tunisian television revived Mu'in's memory with a special programme about him and his poems and their role in the Palestinian struggle. It was not just television, but many articles were also written about him in several newspapers and magazines. On the fourth anniversary of his death, Tunisian radio wanted to interview me at my home and asked if Mu'in's friends could also be present. I welcomed this idea and invited them. It was thought that Abu Iyad would come, but he was in Kuwait and only confirmed on the same day he returned to Tunis. I was told that Chairman Arafat would accompany Abu Iyad, but I didn't tell the radio staff, so it was a big surprise when he arrived. Abu Iyad spoke of Mu'in as a poet, a fighter, and a friend, and talked of his activism and imprisonment, of their work together, as well as about the *Intifada* and the current situation. He also spoke about the years of 1954–55, when Palestinians protested the Johnson proposal that aimed to eradicate Palestinians' right of return and the Palestinian cause. Arafat reminisced about when Mu'in and other community members led Gazans from the south to the north, from Rafah to Beit Hanoon, to protest against the Egyptians and UNRWA, who were complicit with the Johnson proposal.[6] Palestinians in Gaza, Arafat continued, were the masters of the streets then, and they are the masters of the streets now in this *Intifada*. Because of our legendary resistance, he said, we would triumph. Then he recited part of Mu'in's poem "Silence is Death":

> *The truth is not what the* Sultan *or the prince says*
> *It is not the laugh of the big clown*
> *that is sold to the little clown.*
> *If you say it you will die*
> *And if you keep silent you will die*
> *So say it and die.*[7]

Mu'in's friends were so inspired and moved by the words and the meaning of the words and started to recite another poem, "Footsteps":

> *Brother! If they should sharpen the sword on my neck,*
> *I would not kneel, even if their whips lashed*
> *my bloodied mouth*
> *If dawn is so close to coming*
> *I shall not retreat.*
> *I will rise from the land that feeds our furious storm!*
>
> *Brother! If the executioner should drag me to the*
> *   slaughterhouse*
> *before your eyes to make you kneel,*
> *so you might beg him to relent,*
> *I'd call again, Brother! Raise your proud head*
> *and watch as they murder me!*
> *Witness my executioner, sword dripping with my blood!*
> *What shall expose the murderer, but our innocent*
> *   bleeding?*[8]

In Tunis, the Israeli Mossad's policies of assassination and of following our leaders and activists continued, and even increased. We felt really frustrated and angry about the injustices we suffered due to the long arms of the Israeli occupation and the Mossad—which reached everyone and everywhere—as well as the lack of accountability. It didn't matter whether they were leaders or small activists, old or young, civilians or freedom fighters, inside or outside of Palestine. It was a really hard time for us. But we also felt a strong sense of solidarity from the Tunisian government and the people regarding the Palestinian cause.

In 1988, the Mossad assassinated Abu Jihad, the number two man in the PLO, and I read that the Mossad was helped by the sixth fleet of the American Navy in the Mediterranean. They were patrolling international waters, and I believe they were informed about the operation as it couldn't have been done without their knowledge and help, especially because of those rubber boats that were used, the speed of the operation, and then the Mossad unit's return to Israel.[9] I believe that the American fleet watched everything that happened. Israel assassinated Abu Jihad because he supported the *Intifada* in the Occupied Territories and he was a threat to Israel. So, they killed him as part of their aim to kill the *Intifada*. We knew about Abu Jihad's assassination the same night he was killed because we all lived in the same area. The next morning, I went with friends and neighbours to his home, and we saw his blood on the ground and the place where his guard had been assassinated. The street was full of people coming to support Abu Jihad's family and get more news, and also to cry and show solidarity. It was a very gloomy day. Another black day.

When the children left Tunis to study, I was alone and couldn't enjoy the beauty of Tunis because it was connected in my mind to Mu'in's death, but after 1989 I started to visit places. I went to libraries and bookshops and read about Tunisia and its culture and heritage. Tunisians are fond of art exhibitions, and these can be found in almost every corner of their cities and public spaces. They also publish a lot, and I learned about very famous poets and short story writers—some of whose works have been translated internationally. There are youth centres in every district, city, and village, and I was invited to one in Jundubah, a region four hours by car from the capital city of Tunis, where one of Mu'in's plays was performed. That was really wonderful and touched the heart. On the way, I was astonished by the beauty of Tunisia and its deserts, plains, and sea.

I lived in Tunisia for fourteen years and spent the last part taking advantage of its cultural and artistic aspects, and I even attended the Carthage cultural festival every year.[10] One of the years of this festival, Palestinian groups from Nazareth performed and sang Palestinian national songs and recited some of Mu'in's work. In fact, I showed my solidarity to Mu'in, as well as fulfilling my own desires, by attending these cultural events. Once I attended a gathering that included Samih Al Qasim among the poets, and I asked him to recite the poem "Ila Al-Mutamawet: Mu'in Bseiso" (To the one who pretends death, Mu'in Bseiso), which he had written upon Mu'in's death.[11] I cried when I heard Samih, and I always cry when I read these lines:

And you want a grave like those who died
Did we live like those who lived?

And did we die like those who died?
I tried, forgive me
And I swear to God I will not forget them.

In Tunis, the book *Mu'in Bseiso: Bayna al-Sunbulah
wa-al-Qunbulah* (Between the Ear and the Gun) was published
and translated into French (*Mu'in Bseiso: Entre l'épi et le
fusil*).[12] It was about him as a poet, and included his poems,
literature reviews, interpretations, and criticism, as well as
some of his articles.

The Mossad's assassinations continued all over Europe
as well. These operations were shocking for Palestinians
because they showed Israel's opposition to not only their
mere existence and activism, but also to their aspirations
and their dreams to exist in any other place. They assassinated Atif Bseiso in Paris in 1992.[13] We never expected him
to be assassinated and it was a great shock for the family,
especially his wife and very young children. As well as being
Mu'in's relative and close friend, he was very close to my
children. It was also a blow for the PLO. Israel followed
and assassinated Palestinian political activists, leaders, and
writers, wherever they were.

Therefore, Tunis, for me, is connected with such bad
memories of loss and assassinations. In fact, I remember
Beirut more than Tunis, and despite the war and shelling I
have good memories. When I remember Tunis, I remember
bloodshed and assassinations. It doesn't mean that the
Mossad wasn't functioning in Beirut, but we were struggling
side by side with the Lebanese people against Israel and its
constant attacks, invasions, and occupation—which had also
aimed to destroy Lebanon and to deter the Lebanese because
of their support of the Palestinian cause and the Palestinian

people. I still remember the wars, the Israeli invasion, the martyrs, and the siege, but I also remember the people—our neighbours and friends—and the strong relationships we shared. The level of cooperation and coordination in good and bad times, especially during the Israeli invasion, was just incredible. I don't deny that Tunisia and its people helped and welcomed us after we left Lebanon, but I didn't put any effort into making strong connections with the people. Even now, I don't have friends there to phone and ask about their news. I think it was my fear of being uprooted again that had me preoccupied, as well as the loss of everything including friends that we experienced after Beirut. That hindered me from establishing relationships with Tunisians.

In 1991, the Madrid conference was held, with Dr. Haidr Abd Al Shafi, the renowned and respected Gazan leader, and Dr. Hanan Ashrawi, the bright scholar from the West Bank, representing the leadership from Palestine. The Madrid negotiations led nowhere. However, the secret negotiations in Oslo, sponsored by the Norwegian government and attended by delegations from Israel and the PLO, resulted in the Oslo Accords, after which the Palestinian leadership returned to Gaza and Jericho. In Tunis, I saw the pictures of the marvellous welcome of Yasser Arafat to our homeland, and I remembered Mu'in's words: "the place where you put your foot is the place where you put your flag." The important thing was to return to our land because we had spent a long time—twenty-nine years—in exile, and that was enough. The children, especially, wanted to return and start their lives in their homeland.

At that time there was hope, but now Israeli obstacles and aggression have obstructed this hope and dream of peace and freedom. They think that even these fragmented areas

in Gaza and West Bank, which we regained after fifty years
of hard effort and struggle, are too much for us to have, to
possess and enjoy. Sharon, the man who committed horrible
crimes in Gaza back in the 1950s and in 1967, is now hitting
us all—the civilian population together with our leaders
that signed the Oslo agreement—with F16s, with Apache
helicopters, with tanks. They are using all kinds of weapons
against us, and every day there are massacres and martyrs.
And the world is still silently watching. Worse than that,
the Palestinians who are freedom fighters demanding their
rights and the end of military occupation are now portrayed
as terrorists and a threat to Israel's security.

Before the PLO leadership left Tunis for Palestine in 1994,
the president gave a big farewell celebration for them, where
he mentioned Mu'in as the Palestinian poet who encouraged
and called for Palestinian resistance and struggle against
the occupation. It was so kind of him to mention Mu'in and
this touched my heart, so I wrote a letter to thank him and
sent it with a collection of Mu'in's poems and books. Three
months later, I was surprised when a big, beautiful car from
the president's office came searching for my address. I was
given a letter of thanks for the present, and in the letter was
included part of one of Mu'in's poems:

Now you will know that a small window from your
    homeland is open
so you can look from this window to the rest of your land.

6 / Return

IN 1994, after the signing of the Oslo agreement, Tawfiq
returned to Gaza with the first PLO group, and I was given a
Palestinian identity card through a family reunion permit
that Israel approved. It was a weird thing that even after the
peace agreement we still needed permission from the occu-
pier authorities to get back to our homes. I was lucky to get
that permit and I returned in 1995. I wished that Mu'in was
alive and with me to witness the historic moment, as he
always longed to return to his homeland and was waiting for
the moment his feet touched the ground again. But fate
didn't give him this chance. I then returned to Tunis to
collect my belongings so I wouldn't repeat the Lebanon experience. They were shipped in Tawfiq's name because he was
permitted to bring his own things and was on the list of
those that Israel had allowed to return. Although he had
come to Egypt for two weeks to help me collect my belongings, they arrived late in Port Sa'id, and he had to return to
Cairo and go back to Gaza before they came. So, I brought all
of my things to Gaza in 1996 because I knew that it would be
the last move of my life. Many Palestinians sold everything
in Tunis and returned home with nothing, but I didn't want
to sell or leave our memories.

Sahbaa in her home in Gaza City after her return in the 1990s.
(Photo courtesy of Sahbaa's family)

In fact, memories are the only things we bring from the diaspora to our homeland. It is enough to leave the homes that we have built and to be forced to leave and move to another place without leaving our belongings as well. My decision to return was both political and personal: political because it was a direct result of Oslo, and personal because we were returning to our homeland, for which we had waited an excruciatingly long time.

Dalia married in Tunisia in 1994, and in 1997, she came to Gaza for a short visit to collect her identity card as her name was also included on the list of returnees. She then returned to her family in Abu Dhabi. Malika doesn't yet have an identity card. We applied for a family reunion permit for her, and she was accepted last year, but there were too many problems with the process that she didn't have enough time to solve during her vacation. She was sad when she had to leave without getting her card. And then the second *Intifada* erupted in 2000, and everything including civil affairs was frozen as a means of collective punishment, so once again we couldn't follow through with the process. If Dalia now wants to visit Gaza, she needs special permission from Israel. So even with the peace after Oslo, we remain displaced with everyone in different places and have yet to become a united family. My brothers are still in Cairo because it is still the easiest place in the Arab world for Palestinians to live. I have two brothers and four sisters and they have Egyptian residence permits and travel documents, and we don't know when they will be able to return to Gaza. They can come here only for short visits, and only if Israel gives them permission. My brother visited in 1998 and he was only permitted to stay for a month. They are displaced like millions of Palestinians, but they still hold the hope of returning to their homeland.

The first time I applied for a travel document was after 1949 when I wanted to study in Egypt. Then after I married, I exchanged this Egyptian travel document for a Jordanian passport from the Jordanian Embassy in Lebanon, because Mu'in's father had acquired a Jordanian passport in 1958 and his children also had them. When my travel documents were taken in exchange for the passport, I cried for a whole night as I remembered the suffering I had to live through using that document after the conference in Warsaw. Neither the passport nor the document represented me or my nationality, but I understood that the passport would assist my future travels, and I realized that my travel problems were nothing compared to those of Palestinians with other or even no documents. Holding a Jordanian passport helped a lot in this regard, although in the end I was still treated as a Palestinian from Gaza, as that information was written in the passport.

In 1996, I obtained a Palestinian passport issued by the Palestinian National Authority (PNA). I am proud of it and have used it in my travels, and I feel like it has returned part of my identity to me. Not having your own identity card but holding the passport of another country means being questioned, interrogated, and obliged to wait for long periods, and it is possible to be prevented from entering a country or even imprisoned. I am a Palestinian from Gaza who was given Egyptian documents to allow me to travel, and then a Jordanian nationality for ease of movement. How can it be easy to change from one nationality to another when in the end it is not my own? I only felt happy when I was given a Palestinian passport; then I felt that I had an identity, my real identity, the identity that I had lost but dreamt of for many years. With this passport I felt that I regained myself. I can now travel as a Palestinian. The first time I used it, I travelled with Palestinian Airlines in a Palestinian plane flown by a Palestinian pilot with a Palestinian ticket to the United Arab Emirates! It was the happiest trip of my life. It was a wonderful feeling.

Most Palestinian families have the same story—a story of segregation, displacement, dispossession, and constant denial. Ours is not an exception, although many lost their rights before us in the 1948 *Nakba*, and they still haven't been able to return. When my father became very sick in 1949, my mother moved to Cairo with him and the rest of my family for his treatment. After his death, they stayed there for a while until we (my siblings and I) had all finished our education. My mother was travelling between Gaza and Cairo, but then settled in Gaza when I got pregnant to help me with raising my children. Unfortunately, when the war of 1967 broke out, my mother was still in Cairo with my younger brother and sisters, who were studying at Egyptian universities. As a result, they were not allowed by Israel to return and were subsequently stripped of their IDs.

At the end of the war and after occupying the Gaza Strip and the West Bank, Israel denied all the Palestinians who happened to be outside of Gaza at the time of the war— because of work, education, tourism, etc.—their right of return. Hundreds of thousands of Palestinians were stripped of their identity cards and rights of residency, my family included. My sister who resides in Syria also lost her ID, and now I can't see her. In fact, I haven't seen her since 1987. She regularly visits the family in Cairo, but I also couldn't see her the last time because of the multitude of travel problems we Palestinians face in our movements. It's the same with Mu'in's family, who are displaced everywhere. His only sister, Suhair, lives in Cairo, one of his brothers is in Gaza, and the other two are living in Saudi Arabia and in Jordan. My mother died in Cairo while I was there waiting for our belongings to come from Tunisia. She died in the diaspora outside her homeland. It was a difficult time in which I deeply felt the bitterness of the diaspora. Although I still believe that my tragedies are much less than those experienced by other Palestinians, which are generally filled with displacement, alienation, being separated from family, and becoming refugees. The tragedies are the same, but the stories are different.

My father-in-law's grave and Mu'in's brother-in-law's grave are in Tunis, and my mother's and Mu'in's graves are in Cairo, so even in death we are separated. How can I go and visit their graves? I always remember them, especially during *'Eid* when I can't visit their graves, as everyone else does here. They are scattered across borders, and for Palestinians, borders represent the impossible. Yes, Cairo is closer than Tunis, but still I would need to cross borders. So, even in peace we don't have the unity that we dreamed of— in life or in death. We don't know what's going to happen in the future for the rest of us who are still alive.

7 / The High Price of Freedom

NOW WE ARE FIGHTING AGAINST the military occupation of our land on our land, not fighting from Jordan or Lebanon or Tunis. I believe that the only effective way to struggle and fight for the liberation movement is from the inside, not from the outside of Palestine. Now we are on our land and there is no power in the world that can expel us from it. The tragedy of 1948 will not be repeated. Both the Palestinians in exile and those within occupied Palestine have suffered. We, the group outside, suffered because of some Arab regimes, the shadow of the Mossad and their crimes, problems at borders and airports, and a life of instability, while Palestinians in the Occupied Territories suffered from prisons, oppression, interrogations, killings, and all other aspects of living under the military occupation. As I said before, exile is not an alternative for your homeland and will never be. Everyone must be given the choice to return, wherever they are, and whenever they want. All those Palestinians in exile whose land was occupied, homes destroyed, and rights violated by the Zionist project that established Israel must be allowed the choice to return; since Israel agreed with the principle of land for peace, they have to back our rights, including our right of return.

The current *Intifada* calls for liberating the land, returning the rights to the owners, and ending the occupation of 1967. This is what we want. The occupation must end. I still wonder why Israel doesn't want to return our rights to us. Is it a state above the law? Is it a superpower? Is it different from the rest of the world? No, it is the same as any other country. Israel speaks about democracy, but in fact it doesn't have democracy. It is a country built on racism and discrimination, and it doesn't treat its minority citizens well. Take, for example, the Palestinians of 1948, who currently live in Israel and represent about one-fifth of the Israeli population and who are discriminated against with more than fifty laws.[1] Now, after more than half a century of Israeli occupation of Palestinian land, the situation is getting worse. Actually, it started even before the 1948 *Nakba*. It started after World War I and after the defeat of the Ottoman Empire, when the Arab world was divided between France and Britain.[2] But history says as long as people have the will and determination, they will ultimately win and have their rights returned, so here is hoping that we put an end to the occupation. But, of course, there will be many victims and a very high price to pay for freedom. A price we have been paying for way too long.

Actually, I can't understand what Israel wants. Why is it doing this? I don't understand. I don't understand why the United Nations' sanctions were implemented against Iraq and can't be implemented against Israel. We have had our deep roots for thousands of years in Palestine. We are rooted here like the olive and palm trees, the trees that the Israelis are now uprooting, especially in the Deir Al Balah area.[3] That town holds many beautiful memories for me, from when I was young. I am sixty-nine years old now, and I knew Deir Al Balah well, with its tall palm trees that stood like giants in the sky. I used to go there on trips as a student, and as a teacher I took my own students there. It was a very beautiful place, and I still remember the tides coming in between the palm trees. Just like Al 'Arish now, the trees were everywhere in Deir Al Balah, from the town to the beach. The Israeli army has uprooted hundreds of those trees, confiscated the land, and built its army posts, military towers, and the notorious Abu Holi checkpoint. People now can't get to Gaza or to Khan Younis because they frequently close the road.[4] Students and teachers can no longer reach their universities. Even ambulances heading to the hospital are prevented from crossing. When the army closes Abu Holi, life is paralyzed and the Strip is cut into two parts. This closure may last for hours, and sometimes even for days and weeks.

Yesterday, I saw our neighbour's relative, who had come from the Rafah camp to attend the engagement party of her cousin who lives in our building; but then, she could not get back to her house as the checkpoint was closed. This woman has a young baby, two years old. She did not bring him with her as the journey is so difficult, but now she regrets her decision. She was in tears this morning when she headed to Abu Holi. I hope she crosses. She has been going back and forth for the past two days, but with no success in crossing. I wonder, what sin did her baby commit to be separated from his mom at this age? Or what sin did the poor young mother commit so that she is now suffering? This is collective punishment for the Palestinians. Is it only for Israelis to enjoy a healthy motherhood and a good life? Is it only for the Israelis to enjoy the green view and the trees and roses and flowers, and we don't have the same right? Isn't what they occupied and took from Palestine in 1948 enough for them? It is really a strange thing that they want everything and want to deprive us of everything. Why do they have the right to bring Jewish people from all over the world to our land, and yet don't give us the right to return to our homes and lands? Our land is occupied, so what does the world expect from us? To accept and welcome the occupation and not resist?

When I look at the sea and the darkness that covers it, I feel very sad. This sea was always shining and lit by Palestinian ships, boats, and fishermen. Why does Israel prevent us from using the sea, a gift from God? Does the Mediterranean Sea belong to them also? Is it registered in Israel's name? How come we live on the Mediterranean shore and we can't fish because this endangers Israel's sense of security? Every country in the world situated by the sea has the right to fish, but in Gaza, only a small area was specified in the agreement for fishing, and even these parameters are violated by Israel.[5] Palestinians do not even have the right to enjoy the beach or the sea because a few thousand illegal Israeli settlers occupy the shore.[6] The security of these settlers and colonizers requires the deprivation of hundreds of thousands of Palestinians in Gaza, to stop them from reaching and enjoying their beach, so that even enjoying God-given nature is impossible.

Israel, which occupied the West Bank, the Gaza Strip, and East Jerusalem, is the only colonizer that remains in the world. African nations and Latin American countries have achieved their freedom. Colonization has gone from the world, but as I said earlier, Palestinian people are like the phoenix that rises from the ashes. When Israel tries to hit Palestinians strongly, they will not submit to its rule. There have been many martyrs who have lit the way before, and they will be followed by many more who will carry the torch to light the road of freedom. We know that the fight for freedom is very harsh and involves a heavy cost. They want to ensure their existence and security by any means, even at the expense of killing another nation, and we are trying to prove our right to this land in front of a silent world, using every possible means. Unfortunately, the Soviet Union, which supported national freedom movements across the world, has collapsed, so now there is only one superpower. The occupation now tries to prevent Palestinian resistance, whether by stones or words.

My wish is for Palestine to attain its freedom and become an independent state with Jerusalem as its capital, and to achieve the dream of Yasser Arafat, which is the dream of all Palestinians: liberation. I wish to live in peace like other people in the world, with full sovereignty and secure borders under a Palestinian leadership, whether on the land or the sea or in the air. In my opinion, Palestine should be a democratic country where everyone can live, but the West planted Israel as a colonizer in the middle of the Arab world. They want to exploit all the Arab resources—the oil, gas, water, and land—and also want to anchor themselves in the heart of the region due to its very strategic location. The West, led by the US, has their own interests, with very strong imperialist tones. We really do live in the worst time for the Palestinian cause and the situation in general in the Arab world. The Arab countries are controlled by dictatorship regimes that are fully supported by the US, and their interests are connected to them. The Arab countries have declared that they believe in peace as a strategic choice. We also believe in peace, but at the same time we don't believe in surrender.

We want peace and we want to live in real peace—one that is based on rights, not surrender. We want the Israeli occupation to withdraw to the borders of 1967.

I don't wish to destroy the Israeli state and I don't call for this, but I want to live together, everyone within secure borders and with full sovereignty. Why should we fight each other? Why do we have to be enemies? We are against the Holocaust committed by Hitler against Balkans, Romanians, Poles, Czechoslovakians, and Gypsies. We are also against the Holocaust and the horrible crimes committed against the Jews in Europe, and we fully identify with them and with their pain. But we were not responsible for the Holocaust nor were we partners in it, and we didn't support it, so why does this guilt have to fall on us, the Palestinians? It is very strange how the world thinks. It's very strange that we have to pay the price of this guilt and of crimes we have not committed, and the world approves of that. Israel has committed and is still committing crimes against Palestinians; just imagine, they are now (in this *Intifada*) demolishing buildings with people still inside of them.[7]

Israel has to learn from history. Germany and Hitler were defeated because the kind of racism that Hitler represented couldn't work. Many kings and rulers committed crimes against their people and also against other peoples, and the time came when they were overthrown. We believe that this happens to any unjust government or ruler, and if it doesn't happen in our time, it will happen in the time of our children or their children. This barbaric policy based on massacres and bloodshed that the Israeli government has adopted against a civilian population, and against people who were thrown off their land after it was stolen from them, will never last. This is history. They are on the way

to their end and a day will come when they will be beaten.
Israel wants to empty Palestine and create a pure Jewish
state, a state of one religion, which is why they bring Jews
from all over the world to live in Palestine and at the same
time prevent Indigenous Palestinians from returning to their
own lands and homes. This is the peak of racism. But they
will not succeed. They try in all ways to find evidence for
their existence, their right to be here. They try to use history
and religion from three thousand years ago to justify their
existence in Palestine. This means that we should also return
to and control Al Andalus, because Arabs were there once
and controlled it for hundreds of years. It also means that
the Roman and Persian empires should return to the places
they controlled because they were there once, and also the
Ottoman Empire, Britain, and the colonialist regimes. It is
impossible to turn back history. The British controlled an
empire where the sun never set, but a time came when the
sun did set. The Americans are now masters of the world, but
one day another country will take its place.

I wish to live in a free Palestinian state, but I know that
this is a distant wish and it will not happen in my lifetime. It
might happen in the time of my children or grandchildren.
I believe that our struggle for freedom is long term. But
everyone has aspirations and dreams, and without them we
cannot live. Now the world is beginning to sympathize with
the Palestinian cause, but it is only a start. We understand
that more time is needed to create practical steps to support
us. We know that America supports Israel and doesn't
support us. But if America realized that its interests worldwide might be threatened because of this unjust and harmful
position, it might change its attitude and help to find a just
solution for our problem. This might or might not happen,

but I don't believe that the solution will come from America. We, the Palestinians, have the legitimacy and the rights, and we must always continue to raise the question of our rights in international arenas. We also need to look for other global venues to help end this world conspiracy of silence.

Sharon's government, as with previous Israeli governments, is committing the same massacres, and they call it self-defence. So, what shall we call our struggle against the occupation, and our ways of defending ourselves? They call it terror. On television, Dick Cheney, the vice president of the most powerful country in the world, which calls itself a democratic and just nation, justified the occupiers' killing of people under occupation, calling it self-defence. In fact, he wants to justify state terror that acts through infiltration and assassination. We are people under occupation who are struggling for our rights. We waited for our rights and they never came, and now we are confronted by Sharon's planes from the air, his tanks from the ground, and his gunships from the sea. Doesn't the world know that we are under military occupation and that international law gives us the right to defend ourselves—or is it the opposite? Israel is very clever at turning the laws upside down. They call us terrorists and they call the Israeli state's terror self-defence. If this continues, they will spread terror throughout the world, because a war can be ended with an agreement, a just agreement between two parties, but terror cannot be ended. What do you call this? This is state terror. It targets Palestinian areas indiscriminately, using all kinds of weapons. I wonder how their pilots and tank drivers can open fire and kill civilians. Don't they have parents, families, and children? Which law gives them the right to target civilians, and to shell them from the sea, the land, and the air?

I believe that Palestinians committed a terrible mistake when they cancelled some paragraphs in the Palestinian Charter during Clinton's visit to Gaza. That cancellation should have contained conditions because neither America nor Israel can be trusted. Agreements have been signed before by the Israeli government, supported by America, and not implemented. All Oslo agreements must be implemented, and international observers should come and monitor the implementation of these agreements. Now the Clinton administration, which was a government supportive of and loyal to Israel, is gone, but the conflict remains and has become even more complicated because of the blind American support of Israel. We think that Israel is trying to find an alternative Palestinian leadership now that it is ready to concede rights. They have tried this game before and failed, and the demands for rights from an alternative leadership that Israel might try to create will not be less than the demands of the PNA. Perhaps such an alternative leadership would seek even more rights for Palestinians, as the Oslo Accords led by the PNA in the eyes of many Palestinians did not meet the minimum demands of Palestinians.

We can say that the PNA has achieved many positive things, but we should also admit that there have also been many issues, concerns, and setbacks. They are not angels. Their leadership is mostly military, and it is very difficult to change to a civilian leadership in a short time. There have been a lot of mistakes. The positive thing, however, is that the PNA made a homeland for Palestinians. Before, there was nothing called a Palestinian homeland. Yes, it is a small part of the original homeland, but it is a start. Yes, there is no sovereignty or the independence that we dreamed of, but it is a start, or so we hope. It is like an address for all

Palestinians in the diaspora, and the rest of the world knows that now there is a Palestinian entity. Their leadership is the only legal representative of the Palestinian people, and we know they have committed many mistakes during the past eight years, but this happens all over the world. Financial mismanagement, corruption—it even happens in Israel. We know that the seat of power is very attractive and that the one who sits on it doesn't like to leave. Look at President Suharto in Indonesia. He ruled from that chair for thirty-five years, but in one day the people threw him out and prevented him from returning. So, the Authority will not last, because rulers are always changed by the will of the people.

What we want is the full and just implementation of the United Nations resolutions concerning Palestine. Israel was established by a UN resolution that also provided for the right for a Palestinian state, side by side with Israel, but half of Palestine, their share in the UN partition plan, wasn't enough for them. They wanted more. They wanted all of Palestine. I personally believe that the responsibility for what happened in Palestine rests with Britain, whose Balfour Declaration promised the Jews Palestine, and in which the Zionists claimed that Palestine was a land without people, to be given to a people without land. Britain helped the Zionists to establish their state by taking over our land.

I wonder how the British could promise our land to other people, how they considered that Palestine was a land without people and should be given to other people who didn't have any right to be here. We are the native people of this land; we are the owners of this land; we have lived here for hundreds and thousands of years; we have never left this land; and our history is in this land. The British knew this very well. Colonial Britain is fully responsible for what happened to us because of the Sykes-Picot Agreement and its division of the Arab world, and up to now we have suffered.[8] Israel denies us our rights and our homeland that we were forced to leave, and we still have the legal papers to prove this. We still have the keys to our homes. The British government has in its records all the information about our properties, lands, homes, farms—everything. They have all sorts of documents that prove our right to the land, even with names, stamps, and signatures; in other words, formal documents exist. We were thrown off of our land and made into refugees, and the British government knows this very well. Why doesn't it help us to get back our rights, especially with the documents and proof it has in its archives? Why is it only watching and not moving a single step to return our rights? Why does the world pretend that it doesn't see or hear? Why does it keep silent, and why doesn't it move to help Palestinians?

Palestinians will remain on their land. And, God willing, all the Palestinian refugees in the diaspora will be able to return to their homeland. The former Israeli prime minister, Rabin, said that he wished one day he could open his eyes and find Gaza sinking into the sea. Rabin is now dead, actually killed by a right-wing Israeli settler, but Gaza and its people are still resisting. Gaza will not disappear because there is a national will to stay here on our land and a strong faith in the justice of our cause. They can't defeat the will of our people. Now, no power in the world will force us to leave Gaza, Nablus, Ramallah, or Bethlehem. What happened before, in 1948, will not be repeated. We will stay here on our land, and we will not leave or be forced to leave, whatever happens. This is our decision. Even if Israel came with all its might and told me that I was a returnee who came with the Palestinian National Authority and ordered me to leave, I would refuse. I am not afraid of them. I am an Indigenous Palestinian born in Gaza, and I have the full right to be here, and no one can deny me this right. Those settlers who are illegally occupying our land in Gaza and the West Bank, in violation of international law, are the ones who don't have the right to be here. Not me. Please leave, and let us live peacefully on our land. You can arrest, imprison, or torture us, but we will not leave or surrender.

In this *Intifada*, Israel continues to hit our organizations and community centres, destroy our infrastructure, and assassinate our leaders, but even this will not deter the Palestinian people from seeking their rights. As we say in our proverb, *rights will never be lost as long as they have seekers who demand them*. It is our right to have our freedom. We will never surrender these rights, and we will keep demanding them. Israel always speaks about their security, and I say to them, if you want peace and security, you have to give back our rights and acknowledge the Palestinians' right of self-determination. To accept it and live side by side. Palestine has enough room for everyone, regardless of their religion or sect.

Giving back our rights is the shortest way to peace, but assassinating our leaders, bombing our homes, and using all kinds of modern weapons will not give you security, and will not bring an end to the Palestinian cause. Neither you nor America can do this, not now nor in a thousand years.

Chronology of Events in Palestine

1516–1917

Palestine incorporated into the Ottoman Empire under Selim I on August 24, 1516, with its capital in Istanbul.[1]

1897

AUGUST

First Zionist Congress convened in Switzerland from August 29 to 31. It issues the Basel Programme calling for the establishment of "a home for the Jewish people in Palestine." It also establishes the World Zionist Organisation to work to that end.

1914

JULY–AUGUST

Outbreak of World War I as Austria-Hungary declares war on Serbia on July 28 and Germany declares war on Russia and France on August 1 and 3, respectively.

OCTOBER–NOVEMBER

The Ottoman state enters the war on the side of Germany when it begins a naval attack on the Russian Black Sea ports on October 29. Russia declares war four days later.

1916

MAY

Sykes–Picot Agreement is secretly signed, dividing Arab provinces of the Ottoman Empire between Britain and France.

1917

NOVEMBER

British Foreign Secretary Arthur James Balfour sends letter (Balfour Declaration) to Baron de Rothschild on November 2, pledging British support for the establishment of a Jewish national home in Palestine.

1918

SEPTEMBER

Palestine is occupied by Allied forces under British General Allenby.

OCTOBER

End of World War I on November 11, with the signing of the Treaty of Versailles.

1920

JULY

British civilian administration is inaugurated on July 1. Sir Herbert Samuel is appointed first High Commissioner.

1921

MARCH

Founding of *Haganah* (defence), the Zionists' illegal underground military organization.

1922

JULY

On July 24, the League of Nations Council approves Mandate for Palestine without consent of Palestinians.

1923

British Mandate for Palestine comes officially into force on
September 28.

1929

AUGUST

Serious unrest occurs centring on al-Buraq Wall, also known as
the Wailing Wall, a site that holds significance for both Jews and
Muslims in the heart of old Jerusalem. In June 1930, the League of
Nations sends a fact-finding committee to investigate the reasons
behind the uprising. After five months of investigations, the
committee concludes that the area around the wall is an Islamic
endowment, but that the Jews can continue their prayers at the
wall with certain restrictions.

1935

OCTOBER

Irgun Zvai Leumi (National Military Organization), *Irgun* or IZL for
short, founded by Revisionist groups and dissidents from Haganah,
advocates a more militant policy against Palestinians.

1936

MAY

Great Palestinian Rebellion begins in April with the killing of two
Jewish people and a general strike.

AUGUST

On August 25, Lebanese guerrilla leader Fawzi Al Qawuqji enters
Palestine, leading 150 volunteers from Arab countries to help fight
the British.

1939

OCTOBER

The Stern Gang, or *Lochemay Herut Yisra'el* (LEHI; Fighters for the Freedom of Israel), is formed by dissident IZL members led by Avraham Stern.

1942

Formation of the Free Officers by Abd Al Nasser and others. This occurred in steps.

1944

JANUARY

Stern Gang assassinates Lord Moyne, British Minister of State, in Cairo.

1947

MAY

Appointment of eleven-member Special Committee on Palestine (UNSCOP) on May 15, with its first meeting on May 26.

SEPTEMBER

Arab League denounces UNSCOP partition recommendation on September 16.

Arab Higher Committee rejects partition on September 30.

OCTOBER

Jewish Agency accepts partition on October 4.

NOVEMBER

Partition Plan passed by UN Resolution 181 on November 29.

On November 30, Haganah calls up Jews in Palestine aged 17–25 to register for military service.

DECEMBER

Arab League organizes Arab Liberation Army (ALA), a voluntary force of Arab irregulars under guerrilla leader Fawzi Al Qawuqji, to help Palestinians resist partition, at a meeting on December 8.

1948

APRIL

Irgun, IZL, and Stern Gang, led by Menachem Begin and Yitzhaq Shamir, massacre 245–250 inhabitants of Deir Yassin village near Jerusalem on April 9.

MAY

British Mandate ends on May 15. Declaration of State of Israel comes into effect on May 14.

The US and USSR recognize the State of Israel on May 15 and 17, respectively.

UN Security Council appoints Count Folke Bernadotte as its mediator in Palestine on May 20.

Al Nakba begins on May 15.

JUNE–JULY

First Truce in the Arab-Israeli War lasts from June 11 to July 8.

JULY–OCTOBER

Second Truce is ordered by the UN Security Council on July 18 and lasts until October 15.

SEPTEMBER

UN mediator Count Bernadotte is assassinated in Jerusalem by Stern Gang on September 17.

DECEMBER

Israel Defence Forces (IDF) brigade attack on isolated Egyptian forces in Faluja pocket is repulsed.

UN General Assembly passes Resolution 194 (III) on December 11, declaring the right of Palestinian refugees to return.

1949

FEBRUARY

Israeli–Egyptian Armistice is signed on February 24: Egypt keeps coastal strip Gaza-Rafah and evacuates Faluja pocket.

1950

APRIL

On April 24, 1950, the Jordanian parliament officially declares the Unification of the West Bank and the Kingdom of Jordan, the Egyptian–Israeli Armistice Agreement is signed, and the territory now officially known as the Gaza Strip is placed under Egyptian military and administrative rule. While preventing political expression and organization, Egyptian policy preserves the Strip's Palestinian identity, keeping it separate from Egypt as a "Palestinian entity" pending implementation of the relevant UN resolution.

MAY

UN General Assembly establishes the UNRWA (UN Relief and Works Agency) based on Resolution 302 of December 8, 1949.

1951

SEPTEMBER

Yasser Arafat reorganizes the Palestinian Students' Union in Cairo.

1952

JANUARY

British along the Canal Zone attack an Egyptian police post in the city of Ismailia on January 25 and kill fifty Egyptians.

On January 26, more than 750 business establishments burn in Cairo, with thirty people killed and about a thousand injured.

Egyptian Revolution by the Free Officers, which overthrows the monarchy on July 23.

1953

AUGUST

Sharon, the Israeli commander of the UNIT 101, attacks Al Bureij camp in eastern Gaza and kills approximately forty Palestinians.

1954

JULY

British sign a treaty to evacuate their forces from Egypt.

1956

JULY

President Nasser nationalizes the Suez Canal on July 26.

OCTOBER

On October 29, 1956, the tripartite (Britain, France, Israel) invasion of Egypt—the Suez War—is launched. Israel occupies the Gaza Strip (declaring it to be an "integral part of the historical Jewish past") until March 7, 1957, when it is forced to withdraw by the United States and (to a lesser extent) the USSR. The four-month occupation was marked by clashes with the local population and is best remembered by Gazans for IDF "screening operations" in search of men involved with the *Fedayeen*; close to five hundred Palestinian civilians were killed in these operations, and scores of Palestinian fighters were summarily executed. In all, the IDF is estimated to have killed between 930 and 1,200 Palestinians before withdrawing from the Strip.

NOVEMBER

Israel occupies Gaza and most of the Sinai by November 2.

Israel commits a massacre in Khan Younis on November 3.

1957

MARCH

Israel withdraws from Sinai and Gaza by March 6–7. UN Emergency Force moves in simultaneously.

1959

JANUARY

Fatah is established by Yasser Arafat and associates.

JUNE

UN Secretary General (Hammarskjold) puts forth proposal A/4121 for the absorption of Palestinian refugees by the Middle Eastern states on June 15.

1962

OCTOBER

Johnson Plan for Palestinian refugee problem is proposed.

1963

JANUARY

First office is opened by Fatah in Algeria, headed by Khalil Al Wazir (Abu Jihad).

1964

JUNE

Palestine Liberation Organisation (PLO) is founded on June 1, with Ahmad Shuqeri as its first chairman.

1967

JUNE

Six Day War lasts from June 5 to 10. Israel begins military occupation of the West Bank and Gaza Strip of Palestine, as well as Sinai of Egypt and Golan Heights of Syria.

NOVEMBER

UN Security Council endorses Resolution 242 on November 22, calling on Israel to withdraw its army from the territories occupied in the 1967 war.

DECEMBER

Popular Front for the Liberation of Palestine (PFLP) is established, led by George Habash.

1970

SEPTEMBER

Military confrontation occurs between Jordanian army and Palestinian guerrillas ("Black September"), after Palestinian guerrillas hijack four planes on September 6 and 9. Two thousand Palestinians are killed and PLO leadership and troops are expelled from Jordan. PLO sets up new bases in Beirut.

Gamal Abd Al Nasser dies on September 29.

1971

DECEMBER

UN General Assembly Resolution 2787 recognizes the right of Palestinians to struggle for the recovery of their homeland on December 6.

1972

JULY

Ghassan Kanafani, a writer and a member of the Political Bureau of the PFLP, is killed when a bomb explodes in his car on July 8.

OCTOBER

PLO representative Wael Zwaiter is shot and killed in Rome on October 16.

1973

APRIL

Israeli raids in Beirut on April 10 result in the murder of three Palestinian resistance leaders: Kamel Nasser, Kamal Adwan, and Abu Yusuf Al Najjar.

OCTOBER

October or Yom Kippur War begins on October 6. Egypt and Syria fight to regain the Arab territories occupied by Israel in 1967.

UN Security Council Resolution 338 is adopted on October 22, and calls for an immediate ceasefire, the implementation of Security Council Resolution 242 (1967) in all its parts, and negotiations for peace in the Middle East.

1975

APRIL

The 1975–1976 civil war in Lebanon starts on April 13.

1978

MARCH

The Israeli army attacks southern Lebanon on March 14–15, throwing 25,000 troops into a full-scale invasion, leaving scores of Lebanese villages devastated and seven hundred Lebanese and Palestinians, mainly civilians, dead.

SEPTEMBER

On September 17, Carter, Begin, and Sadat sign the Camp David Accords, which propose a settlement of the Middle East conflict and a framework for the conclusion of an Egyptian-Israeli peace treaty.

1981

JULY

Israeli jets bomb PLO targets in Beirut on July 17, killing more than three hundred people.

1982

JUNE

On June 6, Israel invades Lebanon with an estimated 100,000 troops.

AUGUST

The evacuation of PLO troops from Lebanon begins on August 21, as about four hundred troops board a ship to Cyprus.

SEPTEMBER

President-elect Bashir Gemayel and forty followers are killed in Beirut on September 14, a few days before his inauguration.

Over two thousand Palestinian refugees are slaughtered in the Sabra and Shatila refugee camps in Beirut on September 16.

1984

JANUARY

On January 11, the World Zionist Organisation executive body rejects the nomination of former Israeli Defence Minister Ariel Sharon as director of the Israeli immigration programme, citing his role in the massacre of civilians at the Sabra and Shatila refugee camps.

1985

MAY

On May 20, in agreement with Palestinians, Israel exchanges 1,150 Palestinian prisoners for three Israeli soldiers captured during the invasion of Lebanon.

OCTOBER

Israel bombs the Tunisian headquarters of the PLO on October 2, killing more than sixty people, in retaliation for the September 26 killing of three Israelis in Cyprus.

1987

JULY

Israeli military authorities ban Palestinians from fishing in the Gaza Strip area for an indefinite period.

DECEMBER

The *Intifada* begins on December 9. In Gaza, four Palestinians are killed and at least seven are injured when an Israeli truck collides with two vans of Palestinian workers returning from work in the Jabalya district of Gaza.

1988

JANUARY

On January 19, Israeli Defence Minister Yitzhak Rabin announces a new policy for dealing with the *Intifada*: "Force, might, beatings."

APRIL

On April 12, Major General Ehud Barak, deputy Chief of Staff, states that 4,800 Palestinian activists are being held in Israeli prisons, including nine hundred in administrative detention.

Palestinian leader Abu Jihad (Khalil Al Wazir) is assassinated at his home in Tunis on April 16.

In a report on April 17, *The Washington Post* reports that the Israeli cabinet approved the assassination of Abu Jihad (Khalil Al Wazir), and that the operation was planned by the Mossad and Israel's army, navy, and air force.

DECEMBER

During the first year of the *Intifada*, 318 Palestinians are killed, 20,000 wounded, 15,000 arrested, 12,000 jailed, and 34 deported, and 140 houses are demolished. Eight Israelis—six civilians and two soldiers—are killed.

1989

JULY

On July 12, economic adviser to the Chief of General Staff and Director of the Defence Ministry's Budget Department estimates that the cost of fighting the Palestinian uprising is expected to reach approximately 1 billion New Israeli Shekel by the end of the current fiscal year, in March 1990.

1990

MAY

Israeli gunman massacres seven Palestinian workers and injures scores of others at Rishon Lezion near Tel Aviv on May 20.

AUGUST

Iraqi troops invade Kuwait on August 2.

SEPTEMBER

Israeli military authorities raze twenty-six shops and seven homes, and seal four buildings in the Bureij refugee camp in response to the killing of an Israeli soldier.

1991

JANUARY

On January 14, the PLO's second top-ranking official, Abu Iyad (Salah Khalaf), is assassinated in Tunis. Abu al-Hol (Hay Abu al-Hamid) and Abu Mohammed (Fakhri al-Umari) are also killed.

MARCH

On June 18, the Tel Aviv district court sentences Ami Popper, a cashiered soldier, to seven consecutive life sentences plus twenty years in prison for the shooting to death of seven Palestinians in Rishon Lezion in May 1990.

APRIL

Israel releases 240 Palestinian prisoners.

1992

Israel deports 415 Palestinian activists to Lebanon.

1993

JANUARY

The first round of secret Palestinian-Israeli talks on a draft declaration of principles in Norway begins on January 22.

SEPTEMBER

Chairman Arafat and Prime Minister Rabin exchange letters of mutual recognition on September 9.

The Israeli-Palestinian declaration of principles, also referred to as Oslo, is officially signed at the White House by Peres and Mahmoud Abbas on September 13. The declaration provides for a five-year transitional period of limited Palestinian self-rule to begin in Gaza and Jericho, after which final status talks (Jerusalem, refugees, settlements, borders) for a permanent settlement are to be held. The agreement affirms that the West Bank and the Gaza Strip constitute a single territorial unit.

1994

MAY

The Gaza–Jericho Autonomy Agreement (Cairo Agreement) is signed on May 4, outlining the first stage of Palestinian autonomy—in Gaza and Jericho—including Israeli redeployment and the establishment of a Palestinian self-governing Authority. Israel remains in control of the settlements, military locations, and security matters. The stipulated interim period is to end on May 4, 1999.

The first Palestinian police forces arrive in self-rule areas on May 13.

Chairman Arafat returns to Gaza on July 1, accompanied by a limited number of Diaspora Palestinians, and swears in the first PNA ministers on July 5 at Jericho.

1995

SEPTEMBER

The Interim Agreement on the West Bank and the Gaza Strip (Taba or Oslo II Agreement) is signed in Washington on September 28. It outlines the second stage of Palestinian autonomy, extending it to other parts of the West Bank, divided into Area A (full Palestinian civil jurisdiction and internal security), Area B (full Palestinian civil jurisdiction, joint Israeli-Palestinian internal security), and Area C (Israeli civil and overall security control). The election and powers of a Palestinian Legislative Council are determined. The target date for completion of further redeployment is October 1997, and the final status agreement date is October 1999.

NOVEMBER

Israeli Prime Minister Rabin is assassinated on November 4.

1996

JANUARY

The first Palestinian elections with an 88-member Palestinian Legislative Council are held on January 20, and Yasser Arafat is elected as the first president of Palestine.

1997

JANUARY

The Hebron Agreement (also known as the Hebron Protocol) is signed on January 17, in which Israel agrees to withdraw from 80 percent of the city, but will retain control over an enclave of 450 settlers and 35,000 Palestinians in the city centre.

1998

OCTOBER

The Wye River Memorandum, the agreement for the implementation of the Oslo II Agreement and resumption of final status talks, is signed on October 23. It divides the second redeployment provided by Oslo II into three phases, totalling 13 percent of the West Bank, and includes changes in the PLO Charter, the opening of the Gaza airport and safe passage, a reduction in the number of Palestinian police, and the release of Palestinian prisoners. Subsequently, Israel withdraws from 2 percent of the West Bank, near Jenin, the Gaza airport is opened, and some detainees, mostly criminals rather than political detainees, are released.

1999

SEPTEMBER

The Sharm el-Sheikh Agreement for the implementation of the Wye River Memorandum is signed on September 4. It stipulates Israeli withdrawal in three stages from another 11 percent of the West Bank, the release of 350 Palestinian political prisoners, the opening of safe passages, and the beginning of permanent status talks on September 13, 1999 to reach a framework for a settlement by February 2000 and a final peace agreement by September 2000.

2000

SEPTEMBER

The Al Aqsa *Intifada* erupts on September 28 after Likud opposition leader Sharon makes a provocative visit to Al Aqsa Mosque with maximum security, and with thousands of forces deployed in and around the Old City of Jerusalem.

2001

JANUARY

From January 21 to 27 at the Taba Summit, peace talks between Israel and the Palestinian Authority aim to reach the "final

status" of negotiations. Ehud Barak temporarily withdraws from
negotiations during the Israeli elections.

FEBRUARY
Ariel Sharon is elected as prime minister on February 6 and refuses
to continue negotiations with Yasser Arafat at the Taba Summit.

AUGUST
Abu Ali Mustafa, the General Secretary of the PFLP, is assassinated
on August 27 by an Israeli missile shot by an Apache helicopter
through his office window in Ramallah.

2002

MARCH
The Beirut Summit, held over March 27 and 28, approves the Saudi
peace proposal.

MARCH–MAY
On March 29, Israeli forces begin Operation "Defence Shield," Israel's
largest military operation in the West Bank since the 1967 war.

2003

APRIL
The quartet of the United States, European Union, Russia, and
the United Nations propose a road map to resolve the Israeli-
Palestinian conflict, proposing an independent Palestinian state.

SEPTEMBER
Mahmoud Abbas resigns from the post of prime minister on
September 6.

2004

JULY
On July 9, the International Court of Justice issues an advisory
opinion that the West Bank barrier is illegal under international

law. The United Nations had also condemned the construction of the wall as "an unlawful act of annexation" on September 3, 2003.

NOVEMBER

Yasser Arafat dies at the age of 75 on November 11 in a hospital near Paris, after undergoing urgent medical treatment since October 29, 2004.

2005

JANUARY

On January 9, 2005, Abbas wins the Palestinian presidential elections by a wide margin.

AUGUST–SEPTEMBER

Israel disengages from Gaza and removes its settlements from the Gaza Strip, but retains effective control over air, sea, and land access to the Strip.

2006

JANUARY

Ariel Sharon is incapacitated by stroke on January 4. He dies on January 11, 2014, having never emerged from his coma.

On January 25, the Islamic resistance movement, Hamas, wins the Palestinian elections and beats Fatah, resulting in an international and Israeli boycott of the new Palestinian government and imposing a blockade on the Gaza Strip.

2007

NOVEMBER

On November 27, the Annapolis Conference, for the first time, establishes a "two-state solution" as a basis for future talks between Israel and the Palestinian Authority.

2008/2009

Israel launches a twenty-three-day war on the Gaza Strip on December 27.

2012

NOVEMBER

Israel launches an eight-day offensive on the Gaza Strip on November 14.

On November 29, the UN General Assembly passes a resolution granting the state of Palestine non-member observer status, an upgrade that allows the Palestinians to join UN bodies, such as the International Criminal Court (ICC), to investigate war crimes in Gaza.

2014

On July 8, Israel launches a fifty-one-day offensive on Gaza.

2017

US president Donald Trump recognizes Jerusalem as the capital of Israel on December 6. The move is condemned by most of the world in a vote at the UN General Assembly on December 22.

2018

AUGUST

On August 29, the US State Department ends aid to the Palestinian refugee agency, UNRWA, reversing a policy of support by every US president since it was created about seventy-two years ago as a cornerstone of US support for stability in the Middle East.

MARCH

Mass protests start in the Gaza Strip on March 30 (better known as The Great March of Return), calling Israel to lift the eleven-year illegal blockade on Gaza and to allow Palestinian refugees to return to their villages and towns from which they were expelled back in 1948.

MAY

The US moves its embassy to Jerusalem on May 14 and protests sweep the Gaza Strip met by violent repression from Israel, resulting in the deaths of at least 60 and the injury of 2,770 Palestinians in Gaza.

2019

MARCH

On March 25, US president Donald Trump recognizes the Syrian Golan Heights, occupied in 1967, as part of Israel.

NOVEMBER

On November 18, the US says it no longer considers Israeli settlements on the West Bank to be illegal.

2020

JANUARY

On January 28, the US administration reveals the "Deal of the Century," also called "Peace to Prosperity," a plan that jettisons the two-state solution—the international formula proposed to end the Arab–Israeli conflict. The plan, widely described as an attempt to get Palestinians to trade in their political demands for economic benefits, fails to acknowledge major political issues such as the occupation, the siege of Gaza, illegal settlements, and the refugees.

Notes

PREFACE

1. Rosemary Sayigh, *Voices: Palestinian Women Narrate Displacement* (Al Mashriq, 2005/2007), https://almashriq.hiof. no/palestine/300/301/voices/.

2. Edward Said, *Covering Islam: How the Media and the Experts Determine How We See the Rest of the World* (New York: Pantheon Books, 1981), 154.

FOREWORD

1. Nur Masalha, *The Palestine Nakba: Decolonising History, Narrating the Subaltern, Reclaiming Memory* (London and New York: Zed Books, 2012), 288.

2. "What Golda Meir Said about Palestinians," *New York Times*, October 12, 1993, https://www.nytimes.com/1993/10/12/ opinion/l-what-golda-meir-said-about-palestinians-766493. html.

3. Antonio Gramsci, *Selections from the Prison Notebooks of Antonio Gramsci* (New York: International Publishers, 1971), 418.

4. Edward W. Said, *Covering Islam* (New York: Pantheon Books, 1981), 154.

1. "Where We Work, Gaza Strip," UNRWA, accessed February 11, 2021, https://www.unrwa.org/where-we-work/gaza-strip.

2. BADIL, *Survey of Palestinian Refugees and Internally Displaced Persons 2016–2018*, Vol. IX (Bethlehem, Palestine: BADIL Resource Center for Palestinian Residency & Refugee Rights, 2019), https://www.badil.org/en/publication/press-releases/90-2019/5013-pr-en-231019-55.html.

3. Salman Abu Sitta, *Mapping My Return: A Palestinian Memoir* (Cairo: The American University in Cairo Press, 2016), ix.

4. Ibid.

5. Mahmoud Darwish, "Those Who Pass Between Fleeting Words," *Middle East Report* 154, September/October 1988, https://merip.org/1988/09/those-who-pass-between-fleeting-words/.

6. Eóin Murray, "Under Siege," in *Defending Hope: Dispatches from the Front Lines in Palestine and Israel*, ed. Eóin Murray and James Mehigan (Dublin: Veritas Books, 2018), 30.

7. "The State of the World's Refugees 2006: Human Displacement in the New Millennium," UNHCR, April 20, 2006, https://www.unhcr.org/publications/sowr/4a4dc1a89/state-worlds-refugees-2006-human-displacement-new-millennium.html.

8. United Nations, *Gaza in 2020: A Liveable Place?* August 2012, https://www.unrwa.org/userfiles/file/publications/gaza/Gaza%20in%202020.pdf. See also Bel Trew, "The UN Said Gaza Would be Uninhabitable by 2020—In Truth, It Already Is," *Independent*, December 29, 2019, https://www.independent.co.uk/voices/israel-palestine-gaza-hamas-protests-hospitals-who-un-a9263406.html; Donald Macintyre, "By 2020, the UN Said Gaza Would be Unliveable. Did It Turn Out that Way?" *The Guardian*, December 28, 2019, https://www.theguardian.com/world/2019/dec/28/gaza-strip-202-unliveable-un-report-did-it-turn-out-that-way.

Notes

9. Yasmeen Abu Laban and Abigail B. Bakan, *Israel, Palestine and the Politics of Race* (London: I.B. Tauris, 2019), 29.

10. Mark LeVine, "Tracing Gaza's Chaos to 1948," *Al Jazeera*, July 13, 2009, https://www.aljazeera.com/focus/arabunity/2008/02/2008525185737842919.html; Salman Abu Sitta, "Gaza Strip, the Lessons of History," in *Gaza as Metaphor*, ed. Helga Tawil-Souri and Dina Matar (London: Hurst and Company, 2016), 90.

11. LeVine, "Tracing Gaza's Chaos to 1948."

12. Ilana Feldman, cited in ibid.

13. Benny Morris, *Israel's Border Wars, 1949–1956* (Oxford: Clarendon Press, 1993), 416.

14. Ihsan Khalil Agha, *Khan Yunis wa shuhada'iha* [*Khan Younis Martyrs*] (Cairo: Markaz Fajr Publishing, 1997).

15. Salman Abu Sitta, "Gaza Strip: The Lessons of History," *Palestine Land Society,* 2016, http://www.plands.org/en/articles-speeches/articles/2016/gaza-strip-the-lessons-of-history.

16. Helena Cobban, "Roots of Resistance: The First Intifada in the Context of Palestinian History," *Mondoweiss,* December 17, 2012, https://mondoweiss.net/2012/12/roots-of-resistance-the-first-intifada-in-the-context-of-palestinian-history/.

17. "Israeli Colonies and Israeli Colonial Expansion," (CJPME) Factsheet Series No. 9, *Canadians for Justice and Peace in the Middle East*, 2005, https://www.cjpme.org/fs_009.

18. Zena Tahhan, "The *Naksa*: How Israel Occupied the Whole of Palestine in 1967," *Al-Jazeera*, June 4, 2018, https://www.aljazeera.com/indepth/features/2017/06/50-years-israeli-occupation-longest-modern-history-170604111317533.html.

19. Cobban, "Roots of Resistance."

20. "Israel Declines to Study Rabin Tie to Beatings," *The New York Times*, July 12, 1990, https://www.nytimes.com/1990/07/12/world/israel-declines-to-study-rabin-tie-to-beatings.html.

21. A phrase often used after the signing of the Oslo agreements. "Political Economy of Palestine," *Institute for Palestine Studies*, accessed February 11, 2021, https://oldwebsite.palestine-studies.org/ar/node/198424.

22. Abu Sitta, *Mapping My Return*, 317.

23. Edward Said, cited in Abu Sitta, *Mapping My Return*, 187.

24. Abu Sitta, *Mapping My Return*, 299.

25. James Bennet, "Arafat Not Present at Gaza HQ," *The New York Times*, December 3, 2001, https://www.nytimes.com/2001/12/03/international/arafat-not-present-at-gaza-headquarters.html.

26. Ghada Karmi, "'The Worst Spot in Gaza': 'You Will Not Understand How Hard it is Here' Until You See This Checkpoint," *Salon*, May 31, 2015, https://www.salon.com/2015/05/31/the_worst_spot_in_gaza_you_will_not_understand_how_hard_it_is_here_until_you_see_this_checkpoint/.

27. Ghada Ageel, "Gaza: Horror Beyond Belief," *Electronic Intifada*, May 16, 2004, https://electronicintifada.net/content/gaza-horror-beyond-belief/5078.

28. Dennis J. Deeb II, *Israel, Palestine, and the Quest for Middle East Peace* (Maryland: University Press of America, 2013), 36.

29. Mark Tran, "Israel Declares Gaza 'Enemy Entity,'" *The Guardian*, September 19, 2007, https://www.theguardian.com/world/2007/sep/19/usa.israel1.

30. Indeed, the announcement in early 2020 of the Trump–Netanyahu "deal of the century" now seems to have made Israeli unilateralism a mainstay of US foreign policy in the Middle East. For more details, see Avi Shlaim, "How Israel Brought Gaza to the Brink of Humanitarian Catastrophe," *The Guardian*, January 7, 2008, https://www.theguardian.com/world/2009/jan/07/gaza-israel-palestine; Shlaim's article was also published under "Background and Context," in *Journal of*

Palestine Studies 38, no. 3 (Spring 2009): 223–39, doi:10.1525/jps.2009.xxxviii.3.223.

31. Ghada Ageel, "Introduction," in *Apartheid in Palestine: Hard Laws and Harder Experiences* (Edmonton: University of Alberta Press, 2016), xxx.

32. Ibid., xxvi.

33. "Timeline: The Humanitarian Impact of the Gaza Blockade," *Oxfam*, 2020, https://www.oxfam.org/en/timeline-humanitarian-impact-gaza-blockade.

34. For details, see Sara Roy, "The Gaza Strip: A Case of Economic De-Development," *Journal of Palestine Studies* 17, no. 1 (Autumn 1987): 56–88.

35. Shlaim, "How Israel Brought Gaza to the Brink."

36. "World Bank Warns, Gaza Economy is Collapsing," *Al Jazeera*, September 25, 2016, https://www.aljazeera.com/news/2018/09/world-bank-warns-gaza-economy-collapsing-180925085246106.html.

37. Eva Illouz, as cited and discussed in Ghada Ageel, "Gaza Under Siege: The Conditions of Slavery," *Middle East Eye*, January 19, 2016, https://www.middleeasteye.net/opinion/gaza-under-siege-conditions-slavery.

38. Ghada Ageel, "Where is Palestine's Martin Luther King?" *Middle East Eye*, June 26, 2018, https://www.middleeasteye.net/opinion/where-palestines-martin-luther-king-shot-or-jailed-israel.

39. Trew, "The UN Said Gaza Would be Uninhabitable by 2020."

40. David Halbfinger, Isabel Kershner, and Declan Walsh, "Israel Kills Dozens at Gaza Border as U.S. Embassy Opens in Jerusalem," *The New York Times*, May 14, 2018, https://www.nytimes.com/2018/05/14/world/middleeast/gaza-protests-palestinians-us-embassy.html.

41. Mahmoud Darwish, "Those Who Pass Between Fleeting Words."

42. Edward W. Said, "Invention, Memory and Place," *Critical Inquiry* 26, no. 2 (Winter 2000): 12.

43. Jonathan Adler, "Remembering the Nakba: The Politics of Palestinian History," *Jadaliyya*, July 17, 2018, https://www.jadaliyya.com/Details/37786.

44. Ilan Pappe, *The Ethnic Cleansing of Palestine* (Oxford: One World Publications, 2006), 231; Pappe attributes this term to Meron Benvenisti, *Sacred Landscape: The Buried History of the Holy Land Since 1948* (Berkeley: University of California Press, 2002).

45. As cited in John Randolph LeBlanc, *Edward Said on the Prospects of Peace in Palestine and Israel* (New York: Palgrave Macmilllan, 2013), 44.

46. Sonia Nimr, "Fast Forward to the Past: A Look into Palestinian Collective Memory," *Cahiers de Littérature Orale*, no. 63-64 (January 2008): 340, https://doi.org/10.4000/clo.287.

47. For more details, see Peter M. Jones, "George Lefebvre and the Peasant Revolution: Fifty Years On," *French Historical Studies* 16, no. 3 (Spring 1990): 645-63.

48. "Oral History: Defined," *Oral History Association*, accessed February 11, 2021, https://www.oralhistory.org/about/do-oral-history/.

49. Paul Thompson, *The Voice of the Past: Oral History* (Oxford: Oxford University Press, 1978), 25, https://tristero.typepad.com/sounds/files/thompson.pdf.

50. Alistair Thomson, "Four Paradigm Transformations in Oral History," *The Oral History Review* 34, no. 1 (2007): 52-53.

51. Rosemary Sayigh, "Oral History, Colonialist Dispossession, and the State: The Palestinian Case," *Settler Colonial Studies* 5, no. 3 (2015): 193.

52. Sherna Berger Gluck, "Oral History and al-Nakbah," *The Oral History Review* 35, no. 1 (2008): 68.

53. Edward W. Said, "Permission to Narrate," *Journal of Palestine Studies* 13, no. 3 (Spring 1984): 27-48.

54. Gluck, "Oral History and al-Nakbah," 69.

55. Malaka Mohammad Shwaikh, "Gaza Remembers: Narratives of Displacement in Gaza's Oral History," in *An Oral History of the Palestinian Nakba*, ed. Nahla Abdo and Nur Masalha (London: Zed Books, 2018), 16, https://www.researchgate.net/publication/329130803_Narratives_of_Displacement_in_Gaza's_Oral_History_2.

56. Edward Said, as cited in Alan Lightman, "The Role of the Public Intellectual," *MIT Communications Forum*, accessed February 11, 2021, http://web.mit.edu/comm-forum/legacy/papers/lightman.html.

57. Sayigh, "Oral History," 193.

58. Edward Said, "On Palestinian Identity: A Conversation with Salman Rushdie (1986)," in *The Politics of Dispossession: The Struggle for Self Determination, 1969–1994* (New York: Pantheon Books, 1994), 126.

59. "Nakba's Oral History Interviews Listing," *PalestineRemembered.com*, March 31, 2004, https://www.palestineremembered.com/OralHistory/Interviews-Listing/Story1151.html.

60. Ahmad Sa'di and Lila Abu-Lughod, "Introduction: The Claims of Memory," in *Nakba: Palestine, 1948, and the Claims of Memory*, ed. Ahmad Sa'di and Lila Abu-Lughod (New York: Columbia University Press, 2007), 3.

61. As cited in Lightman, "The Role of the Public Intellectual."

62. Maria Fantappie and Brittany Tanasa, "Oral Historian Rosemary Sayigh Records Palestine's Her-Story in *Voices: Palestinian Women Narrate Displacement*," *Wowwire* (blog), *W4*, September 20, 2011, https://www.w4.org/en/wowwire/palestinian-women-narrate-displacement-rosemary-sayigh/.

63. Isabelle Humphries and Laleh Khalili, "Gender of Nakba Memory," in *Nakba: Palestine, 1948, and the Claims of Memory*, ed. Ahmad Sa'di and Lila Abu-Lughod (New York: Columbia University Press, 2007), 209.

64. Ibid.

65. Ibid., 223.

66. Sayigh, *Voices: Palestinian Women.*

67. Fatma Kassem, *Palestinian Women: Narrative Histories and Gender Memory* (London: Zed Books, 2011), 1.

68. Rosemary Sayigh, *The Palestinians: From Peasants to Revolutionaries* (London: Zed Books, 1979).

69. Sayigh, *Voices: Palestinian Women.*

70. Ramzy Baroud, "Gaza: Resistance through Poetry," *Counter Punch,* June 17, 2016, https://www.counterpunch. org/2016/06/17/gaza-resistance-through-poetry/.

1 GROWING UP IN GAZA

1. Al Wehda Street is one of the three major streets in Gaza City. In 1967, Israel occupied the Gaza Strip. A few years later, and to pacify the resistance movement in the Strip, Sharon, the head of Israel's Southern Command, ordered the demolishing of hundreds of homes in order to make it possible for the military vehicles to get into the narrow streets of Gaza's refugee camps and towns. For more details on these operations, see Eyal Weizman, "The Architecture of Ariel Sharon: Sharon Leaves Behind A Legacy of Construction and Destruction That Has Shaped Today's Israel and Palestine," *Al Jazeera,* January 11, 2014, https://www. aljazeera.com/indepth/opinion/2014/01/architecture-ariel-sharon-2014111141710308855.html.

2. The British Mandate divided Palestine into districts and subdistricts. In 1939, some adjustments were made to the 1924 administrative system and the country was divided into six districts and eighteen subdistricts; all reported to the British High Commissioner based in Jerusalem. The districts included Jerusalem, Gaza, Haifa, Lydda, Samaira, and Galilee.

3. Britain made extensive use of colonies' troops in World War II. Many soldiers who ended up in Palestine were from

colonized countries. For more details, see Matthew Hughes, *Britain's Pacification of Palestine: The British Army, the Colonial State, and the Arab Revolt, 1936-1939* (Cambridge: Cambridge University Press, 2019).

4. Al Saraya, a Turkish term, was used to describe the Turkish government's head offices in Palestine during the Ottoman empire. When Palestine was placed under the British Mandate, Al Saraya in Gaza became the British headquarters. Over the decades that followed, the building became the headquarters for whoever ruled Gaza, including the Egyptian administration (1949-67), the Israelis during their military occupation (1967-94), and finally, the Palestinians after signing the Oslo Agreement (1994). The Al Saraya building was completely destroyed in the 2008-2009 Israeli offensive on Gaza. For more details, see Khaldun Bshara, "The Ottoman Saraya: All That Did Not Remain," *Jerusalem Quarterly* 69 (Spring 2017): 66-77, https://oldwebsite.palestine-studies.org/sites/default/files/jq-articles/Pages%20from%20JQ%2069%20-%20Bshara.pdf; and Khaldun Bshara and Shukri Arraf, *All That Did Not Remain* (Ramallah: Riwaq, 2016).

5. On October 29, 1956, Israel attacked Egypt and occupied the Sinai Peninsula and the Gaza Strip. A week later, Britain and France joined the war and occupied the Suez Canal. This attack is widely known in the Arab world as the "Tripartite aggression." A special UN session was held to discuss the situation. The UN called for a ceasefire, the withdrawal of all foreign forces from Egypt and Gaza, and the establishment of an Emergency Force, UNEF, to oversee the withdrawal. Upon the arrival of the UNEF on December 22, 1956, the French and British left Egypt. The withdrawal of the Israeli troops was completed by March 8, 1957. See United Nations, "Summary," *Middle East—UNEF 1: Background*, https://peacekeeping.un.org/en/mission/past/unef1backgr1.html.

6. Terrified by the large number of Jewish immigrations that threatened the demographic balance and fabric of Palestine and their rights in their own country, and in response to the British policies that permitted that influx of immigrants, Palestinian Arabs revolted in 1936. The revolution that became known as the Great Arab Revolt lasted for three years. A six-month national strike was declared at the beginning of the revolt and national committees were created in every corner of Palestine to fight both the British occupation and the Zionist militia groups. Eventually the revolution was brutally crushed by the British. According to Abu Sitta, at least five thousand Palestinians were killed and nearly fifty percent of all adult men living in the area that is now called the West Bank were injured or jailed. For more details, see Abu Sitta, *Mapping My Return*; Rawan Damen, dir., *Al Nakba* (2008; Qatar: Al Jazeera Arabic; 2013; reversioned by Al Jazeera World to English), documentary film, https://interactive.aljazeera.com/aje/palestineremix/al-nakba.html#/17; and Madeeha Hafez Albatta, *A White Lie*, ed. Barbara Bill and Ghada Ageel (Edmonton: The University of Alberta Press, 2020), xviii.

7. One of the largest cities in historic Palestine, Jaffa, had a vibrant and educated Palestinian middle class. It was a centre for cultural life like Beirut and Cairo, and accommodated the major Palestinian newspapers and publication centres. It housed several cultural centres and cinemas, including the famous Alhamra cinema that was opened in 1937. In addition to screenings, Alhamra became a hub for Arab cultural activity in the 1930s. Famous Arab singers including the Egyptian singer Umm Kulthum performed there.

8. Hammam Al Samra is one of Gaza's five original Turkish bathhouses, and the only one that has survived despite the time that has passed and the wars. According to a sign that is placed at its entrance, the Hammam was restored in 1320 during the Mamluk era/period. The United Nations

Development Program (UNDP), in cooperation with the
Islamic University in Gaza, restored the Hammam in the early
2000s. The Hammam still functions and still holds social
importance, especially for women, as a place where community
members come together to socialize and relax. See "Cultural
Heritage," *UNDP FOCUS* 1 (2004): 11, https://fanack.com/
wp-pdf-reader.php?pdf_src=/wp-content/uploads/2014/
archive/user_upload/Documenten/Links/Occupied_
Palestinian_Territories/UNDP_Focus_2004.pdf.

9. 'Omar Al Mukhtar is Gaza City's main high street and has
lots of shops, cafés, restaurants, banks, and government
centres on both sides. It connects Gaza's Old City with the
Mediterranean. It was named after the Libyan freedom
fighter and hero Omar Al Mukhtar, who fought against Italian
colonization in Libya.

10. Yusra Al-Barbari was one of the leading and grand figures in
Palestinian nationalism. Upon her graduation from Cairo
University in 1949, Yusra started her career as a teacher, then
was promoted to be headmistress, and finally became an
inspector in social studies, her area of expertise. She was on
the first Palestinian delegation to visit the United Nations in
1963, joining civil society leaders Dr. Haydar Abd Al-Shafi and
Ibrahim Abu Sitta. When Israel occupied the Gaza Strip, Yusra
refused to work under the occupation's civil administration,
and she resigned from her job as an inspector. Because of
her political activities and community work, Yusra endured
constant harassment from Israeli authorities, and in 1974 she
was prohibited from leaving the Gaza Strip for several years.
She founded and headed several initiatives and societies,
including the General Union of Palestinian Women and the
Red Crescent Society. For more details, see Jean-Pierre Filiu,
Gaza: A History (Oxford: Oxford University Press, 2014).

11. More details can be found in Anis F. Kassim, ed., *The
Palestinian Yearbook of International Law, 1998–1999*, vol.

10 (The Hague: Kluwer Law International, 2000), 180–90; and Filiu, *Gaza: A History*. The 2007 documentary film from director Ran Edelist, *The Shaked Spirit*, also speaks about the crimes committed in the 1967 war, mentioning the burying of Egyptian soldiers while they were alive. See also James Zogby, "The Sins and Horrors of 1967 Are Alive Today," *The National*, June 17, 2017, https://www.thenational.ae/opinion/ the-sins-and-horrors-of-1967-are-alive-today-1.50209. Four of the narrators of this series give testimonies in their respective narratives about these practices.

12. John Kifner, "Israel Detains 2 In Burial Alive of Palestinians," *The New York Times*, February 16, 1988, https://www.nytimes.com/1988/02/16/world/israel-detains-2-in-burial-alive-of-palestinians.html.

13. For more details on Jenin, see Jonathan Steele, "The Tragedy of Jenin," *The Guardian*, August 2, 2002, https://www. theguardian.com/world/2002/aug/02/israel2; and Ramzy Baroud, ed., *Searching Jenin: Eyewitness Accounts of the Israeli Invasion* (Seattle: Cune Press, 2003).

14. Sharon Weill, "The Targeted Killing of Salah Shehadeh: From Gaza to Madrid," *Journal of International Criminal Justice* (2009): 617–31; John Dugard and John Reynolds, "Apartheid, International Law, and the Occupied Palestinian Territory," *European Journal of International Law* 24, no. 3 (August 2013): 867–913, https://doi.org/10.1093/ejil/cht045.

2 THE 1948 *NAKBA* AND STUDIES IN CAIRO

1. UN General Assembly, *Resolution 194 (III): Palestine—Progress Report of the United Nations Mediator*, December 11, 1948, https://unispal.un.org/dpa/dpr/unispal.nsf/0/ c758572b78d1cd0085256bcf0077e51a. The Resolution states the following in para. 11: "*Resolves* that the refugees wishing to return to their homes and live at peace with their neighbours should be permitted to do so at the earliest practical date, and

that compensation should be paid for the property of those choosing not to return and for loss of or damage to property which, under principles of international law or in equity, should be made good by the Governments or authorities responsible; Instructs the Conciliation Commission to facilitate the repatriation, resettlement and economic and social rehabilitation of the refugees and the payment of compensation, and to maintain close relations with the Director of the United Nations Relief for Palestine Refugees and, through him, with the appropriate organs and agencies of the United Nations."

2. The *Nakba*, which literally translates as "The Catastrophe," refers to the mass exodus and dispossession of at least 800,000 Arab Palestinians from historic Palestine in the course of the 1948 war.

3. While in North America, members of the public become volunteers and then are trained as Scout leaders, in Gaza, schoolteachers receive training and become Scouts, after which they train students and take them on such camping trips. They are called Scout teachers.

4. Umm Kulthum was an iconic Egyptian singer, known as the "Star of the East." She is considered one of the greatest singers in Arab history.

5. The war of 1967 was initiated by Israel and lasted for five days. It depended on a surprise attack that destroyed the Arab air forces on the ground and secured Israel's decisive and quick victory in that war. In the course of five days, it captured massive Arab territories including the Gaza Strip and the Sinai Peninsula, from Egypt; the Golan Heights, from Syria; and the West Bank and East Jerusalem, from Jordan. More Palestinians were expelled in the course of the war. See Jeremy Bowen, "1967 War: Six Days that Changed the Middle East," BBC, June 5, 2017, https://www.bbc.com/news/world-middle-east-39960461.

6. Al Faluja was one of the forty-five villages of the Gaza District. It was situated on high ground, about 30 kilometres northeast of Gaza. The village had strategic value as it was a hub of central roads leading to north and south Palestine. During the 1948 war, an Egyptian unit led by Jamal Abd Al Nasser together with the inhabitants of the village, about 3,140, were trapped in Al Faluja for several months. Eventually, the parties signed the armistice agreement in February 1949, which put an end to the Israeli siege and secured a safe withdrawal for the Egyptian unit. The terms of that agreement were then violated by Israel, which used various sorts of tactics to expel the residents of Al Faluja. According to the UN observers, these tactics included beatings, looting, and attempted rapes. In Walid Khalidi, ed., *All That Remains: The Palestinian Villages Occupied and Depopulated by Israel in 1948* (Washington, DC: Institute for Palestine Studies, 1992), 94-97.

7. In January 1952, and following the murder of about fifty Egyptian policemen by British troops in the city of Isma'iliya, hundreds of businesses, key buildings, and cultural centres were deliberately burned and looted in the capital city of Cairo. Many thinkers and analysts thought that the Fire, as it is called, marked the end of the King's rule in Egypt. Decades after the Fire, little is known about the architect behind the incident. For more details, see Tarek Osman, *Egypt on the Brink* (New Haven and London: Yale University Press, 2010), 39.

8. In February 1946, thousands of students from Cairo University participated in a large demonstration against the British occupation. The demonstration was suppressed violently and ended with a terrible massacre, widely known as the Abbas Bridge Massacre. Many students were shot dead or drowned as the army opened up the moveable Abbas bridge while demonstrators were marching over it. See Heba Helmy, "Streets of Cairo: Nahdet Misr Street, A Reflection of Modern Egypt," *Egypt Independent,*

November 5, 2011, https://ww.egyptindependent.com/
streets-cairo-nahdet-misr-street-reflection-modern-egypt/.

9. The Egyptian army's failures were evident after the 1948
   Arab-Israeli war, and many of the officers, including Jamal
   Abd Al Nasser and General Muhammad Nagib, accused King
   Farouk of abandoning them. In 1949, Abd Al Nasser formed
   the Free Officers group, which became the Free Officers
   Movement. The group's main goals were to topple the King
   and abolish the monarchy, which was allied to the British
   Empire and, in the view of many Egyptians, responsible for
   the defeat in Palestine. To fix this weakness, the Free Officers'
   leadership thought that the regime needed to be cleaned up
   at its roots and branches. On July 23, 1952, the Free Officers
   overthrew the King, and Nagib become the first Egyptian
   president. See Yasmina Allouche, "Remembering the 1952
   Egyptian Revolution," *MEM*, July 23, 2017, https://www.
   middleeastmonitor.com/20170723-remembering-the-1952-
   egyptian-revolution/; and Abu Sitta, *Mapping My Return*, 177.

10. Anwar Sadat was the third president of Egypt, serving from
    the time of his election in October 1970 until his assassination
    on October 6, 1981. For more details on his legacy, see Jon
    B. Alterman, "Sadat and His Legacy: Egypt and the World,
    1977–1997," *The Washington Institute for Near East Policy*, April
    1, 1998, https://www.washingtoninstitute.org/policy-analysis/
    sadat-and-his-legacy-egypt-and-world-1977-1997.

11. The Johnson proposal (1955) was a joint UN and Egyptian
    government project that aimed to settle Gazan refugees in the
    northwest area of the Sinai Peninsula. Palestinian refugees saw
    this as a plan to complete their ethnic cleansing and liquidate
    their cause. The Refugees' committee in Gaza together with the
    active political groups and civil society leaders led the protests
    against the proposal. Many Palestinians were arrested by the
    Egyptian police, including the Gazan Mu'in Bseiso, Sahbaa's

husband, who spent eight years in an Egyptian jail. For more details, see Abu Sitta, *Mapping My Return.*

12. Marion Farouk Sluglett and Peter Sluglett, *Iraq Since 1958: From Revolution to Dictatorship* (New York: IB Tauris, 1990); and Roby Barret, "Intervention in Iraq: 1958–1959," *Middle East Institute*, April 1, 2008, https://mei.edu/publications/intervention-iraq-1958-1959.

13. The Jordanian Communist Party, or JCP, encountered severe repression from the state. Many of its members were jailed. In January 1957, King Hussein removed the parliamentary immunities of the party's elected members and imprisoned many of them. The party's activities were very nearly halted. For more details on King Hussein and Abd Al Nasser's suppression of the communist parties, see Farouk Sluglett and Sluglett, *Iraq Since 1958*, and Barret, "Intervention in Iraq."

14. Abu Sitta, *Mapping My Return*, 12.

3 ARREST AND IMPRISONMENT

1. Abu Sitta, *Mapping My Return*, 120.

4 MARRIAGE AND EXILE

1. The Bar Lev Line was a fortified line of defence of almost 160 kilometres, constructed by the Israeli army along the eastern bank of the Suez Canal in 1968. In 1973, the Egyptian army succeeded in destroying the Bar Lev Line and crossing the Canal. See Baruch Kimmerling, *Politicide: Ariel Sharon's War Against the Palestinians* (London: Verso, 2003), 60.

2. In August 1982, as the result of an agreement negotiated by a special United States envoy, Philip Habib, the PLO leadership evacuated its forces from Beirut and moved its main base of operations to Tunisia. It remained there for twelve years, then relocated to Gaza in 1994 after signing the Oslo agreement. For more info, see Jamil Hilal, "PLO Institutions: The Challenge

Ahead," *Journal of Palestine Studies* 23, no. 1 (Autumn, 1993): 46–60.

3. Ghassan Kanafani was a Palestinian novelist and writer. Born in Acre, Palestine (1936), Kanafani and his family became refugees in 1948 and settled in Syria. Kanafani joined the Popular Front for the Liberation of Palestine (PFLP) and became the editor of its weekly newspaper, *al-Hadaf*, which he founded in 1969. Many of his novels including *Men Under the Sun, Returning to Haifa*, and *All That's Left to You* were translated into different languages. At the age of thirty-six, he was assassinated by the Israeli Mossad in Beirut by a bomb planted under his car. For more details, see Elias Khoury, "Remembering Ghassan Kanafani, or How a Nation Was Born of Story Telling," *Journal of Palestine Studies* 42, no. 3 (Spring 2013): 85–91.

4. Rana Abdullah, "I Knew a Hero Once: My Uncle Mahmoud, in My Memory, 40 Years On," *The Palestine Chronicle*, May 9, 2013, https://www.palestinechronicle.com/i-knew-a-hero-once-my-uncle-mahmoud-in-my-memory-40-years-on/.

5. Israel targeted Palestinian political leaders and activists during the second *Intifada*. In August 2001, Abu-Ali Mustafa, Secretary-General of the PFLP, was assassinated. For more details on Israel's policy of assassination, see Gal Luft, "The Logic of Israel's Targeted Killing," *Middle East Quarterly* 10, no. 1 (Winter 2003): 3–13, http://www.meforum.org/article/515.

6. In April 1975, unknown militiamen opened fire on the Notre Dame de la Deliverance church in the Ain Al Rummaneh, a suburb of East Beirut, killing four people. Two of them were members of the Christian Phalange or Kataeb Party. Accusing Palestinians, the Phalangists opened fire, killing about thirty Palestinian passengers aboard a bus that happened to be passing through Ain Al Rummaneh. For more info on the Lebanese civil war, see Rebecca Burn,

"Absent Memory: A Study of the Historiography of the Lebanese Civil War of 1975-1990" (B.A. thesis, Wesleyan University, 2012), https://pdfs.semanticscholar.org/fb16/4df7ff2daa157025e87906052133485f790f.pdf.

7. Othman Hassan, "Mu'in Bseiso: Quwwit al kalima taqhar jahim al quyood" [Mu'in Bseiso: The power of the word conquers the hell of chains], *Alkhaleej*, May 15, 2018, https://www.alkhaleej.ae/node/pdf/651253/pdf.

8. See H. Aram Veeser, *Edward Said: The Charisma of Criticism* (London: Routledge, 2010), 187; and Rashid Khalidi, *The Iron Cage: The Story of the Palestinian Struggle for Statehood* (Boston: Beacon, 2006).

9. The Shaqif Castle (known as Belfort or Beaufort) is located in a strategic area that provides a view of much of southern Lebanon and northern Palestine. The PLO had held the Castle since 1976. On June 6, 1982, the Castle was heavily shelled by the Israeli army for two days. Eventually it was captured after a fierce resistance in what became known as the Battle of the Shaqif. See Robert Fisk, *Pity the Nation: Lebanon at War* (Oxford: Oxford University Press, 2001), 727.

10. Mu'in Bseiso, *88 Days Behind the Barricades* (*Thamaniya wa thamanoun yowman khalf al matarees*), (Beirut: Dar Al Farabi, 1985).

11. "The Bombing of Beirut," *Journal of Palestine Studies* 11, no. 1 (1981): 218-25, doi:10.2307/2536065.

12. Philip Habib, the US special envoy, hammered out an agreement to end the Israeli invasion of Lebanon, providing for the evacuation of PLO forces from Lebanon and the withdrawal of both Israeli army and Syrian forces from Beirut. The PLO evacuation was to be observed by multinational peacekeeping forces composed of troops from France, Italy, and the US. See Seyom Brown, *Faces of Power: Constancy and Change in United States Foreign Policy from Truman to Obama*, 3rd ed. (New York: Columbia University Press, 2015), 405-20.

13. PLO institutions in Lebanon (1982), Tunis (1985), and the West Bank, including East Jerusalem and Gaza, have been systematically bombed and attacked by Israel since 1967. For more details, see Ihsan A. Hijazi, "Israel Looted Archives of P.L.O., Officials Say," *The New York Times,* October 1, 1982, https://www.nytimes.com/1982/10/01/world/israeli-looted-archives-of-plo-officials-say.html; "Study Says Attacks on Infrastructure in Gaza and West Bank Exact a Human Cost," Nicholas School of the Environment, Duke University, February 18, 2019, https://nicholas.duke.edu/news/study-says-attacks-infrastructure-gaza-and-west-bank-exact-human-cost; and Lizzie Dearden, "Israel-Gaza Conflict: University Hit As Palestinians Endure More Than 200 Strikes in 24 Hours," *Independent*, August 2, 2014, https://www.independent.co.uk/news/world/middle-east/israel-gaza-conflict-university-hit-as-palestinians-endure-more-than-200-strikes-in-24-hours-9644243.html.

5 TUNIS

1. On September 14, 1982, Bashir Gemayel, the newly elected President, at thirty-four years old, was speaking in East Beirut at his Phalangist Party's headquarters when a bomb exploded and killed him. A twenty-six-year-old member of a party that was a rival of the Phalangists was accused of the assassination. For more details, see Bob Woodward, "Alliance with a Lebanese Leader," *Washington Post*, September 29, 1987, https://www.washingtonpost.com/archive/politics/1987/09/29/alliance-with-a-lebanese-leader/ab94dec7-2029-409b-8ebd-cbf954318cc1/?utm_term=.0ce6f06d9a13.

2. On September 1, 1982, President-elect Bashir Gemayel met with Israeli Prime Minister Menachem Begin in Israel, who demanded that Gemayel sign a peace treaty with Israel. Begin threatened that Israel would stay in South Lebanon if the Peace Treaty wasn't signed. Gemayel, who was angered by

Begin's words, refused the offer and returned to Lebanon. He did not change his position. For more details, see Carole Collins, "Chronology of the Israeli War in Lebanon September–December 1982," *Journal of Palestine Studies* 12, no. 2 (Winter 1983): 86–159.

3. Nasim Ahmed, "Remembering the Sabra and Shatila Massacre," *Middle East Monitor*, September 16, 2019, https://www.middleeastmonitor.com/20190916-remembering-the-sabra-and-shatila-massacre/.

4. On October 1, 1985, a unit of the Israeli air force launched a strike on the Hammam Chott, a suburb that is less than 20 kilometres from the Tunisian capital. The targets were PLO chairman Yasser Arafat and other PLO leaders coming in from different neighbouring Arab countries for a meeting. Due to a delay in some leaders' flights, the meeting was postponed to the evening. The strike killed sixty-eight people and injured one hundred Palestinians and Tunisians. For more details, see "32 Years Since Israel Bombed Hammam Chott," *MEM*, October 2, 2017, https://www.middleeastmonitor.com/20171002-32-years-since-the-zionist-bombing-of-hammam-chott/; and Talcott W. Seelye, "Special Report: Ben Ali Visit Marks Third Stage in 200-Year-Old US-Tunisian Special Relationship," *Washington Report on Middle East Affairs,* March 1990, https://www.wrmea.org/1990-march/ben-ali-visit-marks-third-stage-in-200-year-old-us-tunisian-special-relationship.html.

5. Hammam Chott cemetery is the Palestinian national cemetery in Tunisia, where all Palestinians who are not allowed by Israel to be repatriated are buried.

6. In 1954–55, Palestinians demonstrated from Rafah to Beit Hanoon and organized strikes and large-scale demonstrations for nine days straight, taking over the streets of the Gaza Strip. They were led by Palestinian civil society leaders and activists to protest against the Johnson proposal. The Egyptian

authorities couldn't stop the protesters, and the proposal failed. For more details, see Abu Sitta, *Mapping My Return*, 120.

7. The poem in Arabic can be found at Abdul Hamid Al-Qaed, "Glow of Writing: Say it and Die," January 6, 2018, http://akhbar-alkhaleej.com/news/article/1104213.

8. The translation of the poem "Footsteps" from Arabic to English is based on May Jayyusi and Naomi Shihab Nye's translation; see http://palestineupdates.com CJPME footsteps-a-poem-by-muin-bseiso/.

9. In 1988, the Mossad, Israel's secret intelligence service, assassinated Abu Jihad (Khalil Al Wazir), the number two man in the PLO leadership after Arafat. The Israeli cabinet-approved assassination and overall operation were planned and executed by the Mossad, with cooperation from Israel's army, navy, and air force. See the editorial from *The Jordan Times* on the implications of the assassination, published as "The Assassination of Abu Jihad," *Journal of Palestine Studies* 17, no. 4 (Summer 1988): 146–47, doi:10.2307/2537305; and "Abu Jihad Killing: Israeli Censor Releases Commando's Account," *BBC News*, November 1, 2012, https://www.bbc.com/news/world-middle-east-20172511.

10. As the name highlights, the international festival of Carthage takes place at the Roman Theatre of Carthage, located in Carthage, a residential suburb of the Tunisian capital city, Tunis. See Patrick Hunt, "Carthage, Ancient City, Tunisia," *Encyclopedia Britannica Online*, accessed February 10, 2021, https://www.britannica.com/place/Carthage-ancient-city-Tunisia. The festival attracts people from around the world. In 2019, the 55th International Festival of Carthage (IFC) featured a program of music, dance, and performing arts from July 11 to August 20. See "The 55th Festival of Carthage Excites Tunisia," *Atlantico*, July 9, 2019, https://atlanticoonline.com/en/the-55th-festival-of-carthage-excites-tunisia/.

11. To see a copy of the poem in Arabic, see Ataallah Muhajrani, "Ila Al Mutamawit—Samih Al Qasim" [To the dead—Samih Al Qasim], *Alsharq Alawsat*, August 25, 2014, https://aawsat.com/home/article/167221.

12. Mu'in Bseiso, *Mu'in Bseiso: Entre l'épi et le fusil* (Tunis: Lotus, 1988).

13. The PLO security chief, Atif Bseiso, was assassinated in Paris in 1992. It is believed that the assassination was carried out by agents of the Mossad. For more details, see Rone Tempest, "PLO Official Assassinated on Paris Street," *Los Angeles Times*, June 9, 1992, https://www.latimes.com/archives/la-xpm-1992-06-09-mn-182-story.html; and Jonathan C. Randal, "Assassination of PLO Aide Raises Many Questions," *The Washington Post*, July 10, 1992, https://www.washingtonpost.com/archive/politics/1992/07/10/assassination-of-plo-aide-raises-many-questions/c482bb3e-a437-474d-9835-421397ce87bf/?noredirect=on&utm_term=.8785a980fce8.

7 THE HIGH PRICE OF FREEDOM

1. "Discrimination Against Palestinian Citizens of Israel," *Institute for Middle East Understanding*, September 28, 2011, https://imeu.org/article/discrimination-against-palestinian-citizens-of-israel; and Rachel Shabi, "Understanding Israel through its Marginalised Mizrahi Jews," TRT *World,* June 28, 2017, https://www.trtworld.com/opinion/understanding-israel-through-the-marginalised-mizrahi-jews-389035.

2. The borders of the Arab region, including Palestine, were sketched during World War I by two diplomats, the British Mark Sykes and the French Francois Picot, in what became known as the Sykes–Picot Agreement, which was signed in 1916. According to the agreement, the territories captured or inherited from the Ottoman empire would be divided between Britain and France as well as other colonial powers such as

Italy and Russia. See George Antonius, *The Arab Awakening: The Story of the Arab National Movement* (New York: Capricorn Books, 1965).

3. This story was recorded during the second *Intifada*, when Israel bulldozed dozens of *dunumes* (a *dunume* is 1,000 square metres) and uprooted thousands of palm and olive trees to establish the Abu Holi military checkpoint on Salah Al Dein road, the main road in the Gaza Strip. The land was confiscated from the Abu Holi family and the checkpoint was named after them.

4. Karmi, "'The Worst Spot in Gaza.'"

5. Under the Oslo peace agreement, signed between Israel and the PLO in 1993, Palestinian fishermen are allowed to fish in an area of 20 nautical miles (37 kilometres). As part of the Israeli illegal blockade imposed on the Gaza Strip, the Israeli Navy has reduced the fishing zone down to 6 miles, and sometimes to only 3 miles offshore. Due to these restrictions, thousands of Palestinian fishermen are denied their right to access 85 percent of Gaza's maritime areas, which drastically affects their work and livelihood and deprives the two million Palestinian inhabitants of the Strip of their right to water and their traditional diet.

6. This story was recorded before the Israeli deployment from Gaza in September 2005. At that time, Israeli soldiers and settlements occupied 40 percent of Gaza's land and dominated over most modes of access to the beach and to natural resources (e.g., water).

7. Israel has demolished Palestinian houses as a punitive measure since the beginning of the military occupation of the West Bank and Gaza Strip in 1967. The extent of such demolitions has varied over the years. According to the Israeli human rights organization, Btselem, from 1967 to the outbreak of the first *Intifada* in December 1987, Israel demolished or sealed at least 1,387 housing units. In the course of the al-Aqsa

Intifada, Israel renewed its use of house demolitions. As part of this policy, Israel demolished 628 homes from October 2001 to September 20, 2004. Even during the pandemic, Israel has continued to use its policy of home and residential structure demolition. Over the course of 2020 alone, more than 900 Palestinians, half of them children, lost their homes compared to 677 Palestinians in 2019. For more details, see Btselem's summary of its report, *Through No Fault of Their Own: Israel's Punitive House Demolitions in the al-Aqsa Intifada* (Jerusalem, Israel: Btselem, November 2004), https://www.btselem.org/publications/summaries/200411_punitive_house_demolitions; and "Israel Commits a Crime and Paints Palestinians as Lawbreakers: The Homes of 44 Palestinians, Including 22 Children, Were Demolished Yesterday in the West Bank," *Btselem,* November 26, 2020, https://www.btselem.org/press_releases/20201126_44_palesinian_homes_demolished_israel_commits_crime_and_paints_palestinians_as_the_offenders.

8.   For more details on the Sykes-Picot agreement, see Antonius, *The Arab Awakening.*

CHRONOLOGY OF EVENTS IN PALESTINE

1.   The following works were consulted when compiling this chronology of events in Palestine: Walid Khalidi, ed., *All That Remains: The Palestinian Villages Occupied and Depopulated by Israel in 1948* (Washington, DC: Institute for Palestine Studies, 1992); Mahdi F. Abdul Hadi, ed., *Documents On Palestine, Volume I: From the Pre-Ottoman/Ottoman Period to the Prelude of the Madrid Middle East Peace Conference* (Jerusalem: Palestinian Academic Society for the Study of International Affairs, 1997); Said K. Aburish, *A Brutal Friendship: The West and the Arab Elite* (New York: St. Martin's Press, 1998); *PASSIA Diary 1999* (Jerusalem: Palestinian Academic Society for the Study of International Affairs, 1998); *PASSIA Diary 2001*

(Jerusalem: Palestinian Academic Society for the Study of International Affairs, 2000); Ilan Pappe, *The Ethnic Cleansing of Palestine* (Oxford: Oneworld Publications, 2006); Rashid Khalidi, *The Iron Cage: The Story of the Palestinian Struggle for Statehood* (Boston: Beacon Press, 2006); Linda Butler, "A Gaza Chronology, 1948–2008," *Journal of Palestine Studies* 38, no. 3 (2009): 98–121, doi:10.1525/jps.2009.XXXVIII.3.98; "A Lot of Process, No Peace: A Timeline of 20 Years of Post-Oslo Meetings, Agreements, Negotiations and Memorandums," *Perspectives: Political Analyses and Commentary from the Middle East & North Africa* 5 (December 2013), 5–8; Amira Hass, *Drinking the Sea at Gaza: Days and Nights in a Land Under Siege* (New York: Henry Holt and Company, 2014); *PASSIA Diary 2018* (Jerusalem: Palestinian Academic Society for the Study of International Affairs, 2017); "Palestine: What Has Been Happening Since WWI," *Al Jazeera*, May 14, 2018, https://www.aljazeera.com/focus/arabunity/2008/02/20085251908164329.html; Eóin Murray and James Mehigan, eds., *Defending Hope: Dispatches from the Front Lines in Palestine and Israel* (Dublin: Veritas Books, 2019); Chloé Benoist, "'The Deal that Can't be Made': A Timeline of the Trump Administration's Israel-Palestine Policy," *Middle East Eye*, January 28, 2020, https://www.middleeasteye.net/news/deal-cant-be-made-timeline-trump-administrations-israel-palestine-policy; Rashid Khalidi, *The Hundred Years' War on Palestine: A History of Settler Colonialism and Resistance, 1917–2017* (New York: Metropolitan Books, 2020).

Glossary

Al Daraj: A suburb of the Old City of Gaza.

Al Sabra: A suburb of the Old City of Gaza.

Al Saraya: A Turkish term that refers to the government headquarters in Palestine during the Ottoman Empire Era. When
Palestine was brought under the British Mandate, Al Saraya
in Gaza became their headquarters. Over the decades that
followed, the building became the headquarters for whoever
ruled Gaza, including the Egyptian administration (1949-67),
the Israelis during their military occupation (1967-94), and
finally, the Palestinians after signing the Oslo Agreement (1994-
2008). For more details, see Bshara, "The Ottoman Saraya," and
Bshara and Arraf, *All That Did Not Remain*.

Al Sidra: A shrine of a holy man, situated in the Old City of Gaza.

'Arayis: Handmade dolls for which the outline of the bride was
drawn on material, and then cut, sewed, and filled with other
material or whatever was available.

Buqja: A bag made of velvet and covered with silk or embroidery, like a cushion cover, and made especially for public baths.
People carried these bags to show that they were well off.

'Eid: Feast.

'Eidiyyeh: Money given to children on *'Eid* days.

Fanoos (pl. fawanees): Decorative lamp made of bronze or
colourful glass. Children usually carry them, small ones though,
during Ramadan.

Fedayeen (sing. Feda'i): Palestinian resistance fighters. In this book, *Fedayeen* refers to those Palestinians who left their families and homes and were organized and trained and became wanted men to defend their land against enemy attacks.

Hammam Al Samra: The only Turkish public bathhouse in Gaza, of the original five, that continues to function. A sign placed in the entrance of the bath indicates that it was restored by the Mamluk period around the year 1320. Working with the Islamic University in Gaza, the UNDP restored the hammam in the early 2000s. It holds social importance, especially to women, as a place where community members come together to socialize.

Jalabiya (pl. jalabiyaat): Traditional Arab men's dress of a long cotton gown.

Ka'k or **Ka'k al 'Eid**: Date paste enclosed by biscuit dough, which is rolled and joined in a circular shape and cooked, then dusted with icing sugar. Especially popular at *'Eid al Fitr*.

Nakba: The catastrophe, referring to the mass expulsion of Palestinian Arabs from British Mandate Palestine during Israel's creation between 1947 and 1949.

Qersh: Small denominations of Palestinian currency; a qersh was equal to 1/100 English pound of the time.

Ramadan: Islamic holy month, during which there is fasting during daylight hours and a meal at nightfall and before daybreak.

Shatat: The suffering of dispersion, referring to the experience of Palestinians in exile.

Tahenah: Sesame paste.

Tawjihi: Graduating or senior certificate from high school, the results of which determine whether the student is eligible for university study.

Bibliography

Abdo, Nahla, and Nur Masalha, eds. *An Oral History of the*
Palestinian Nakba. London: Zed Books, 2018.

Abdullah, Rana. "I Knew a Hero Once: My Uncle Mahmoud, in My
Memory, 40 Years On." *The Palestine Chronicle*, May 9, 2013.
https://www.palestinechronicle.com/i-knew-a-hero-once-my-
uncle-mahmoud-in-my-memory-40-years-on/.

Abu Jaber, Ibrahim, Wisam Afifi, Maisam Eid, et al. *Jurh Al-Nakba:*
Part 1 [The Wound of Nakba: Part 1]. Um Al-Fahem: Centre of
Contemporary Studies, 2003.

Abu Laban, Yasmeen, and Abigail B. Bakan. *Israel, Palestine and the*
Politics of Race. London: I.B. Tauris, 2019.

Abu Sitta, Salman. "Gaza Strip: The Lessons of History." *Palestine*
Land Society. 2016. http://www.plands.org/en/articles-speeches/
articles/2016/gaza-strip-the-lessons-of-history.

———. *Mapping My Return: A Palestinian Memoir*. Cairo and New
York: The American University in Cairo Press, 2016.

Abu Sharif, Bassam. *Arafat and the Dream of Palestine: An Insider's*
Account. New York: Palgrave Macmillan, 2009.

Adler, Jonathan. "Remembering the Nakba: The Politics of
Palestinian History." *Jadaliyya*, July 17, 2018. https://www.
jadaliyya.com/Details/37786.

Ageel, Ghada, ed. *Apartheid in Palestine: Hard Laws and Harder*
Experiences. Edmonton: University of Alberta Press, 2016.

———. "Gaza: Horror Beyond Belief." *Electronic Intifada*, May 16, 2004. https://electronicintifada.net/content/gaza-horror-beyond-belief/5078.

———. "Gaza Under Siege: The Conditions of Slavery." *Middle East Eye*, January 19, 2016. https://www.middleeasteye.net/opinion/gaza-under-siege-conditions-slavery.

———. "Introduction." In *Apartheid in Palestine: Hard Laws and Harder Experiences*, edited by Ghada Ageel, xxv–xliv. Edmonton: University of Alberta Press, 2016.

———. "Where is Palestine's Martin Luther King?" *Middle East Eye*, June 26, 2018. https://www.middleeasteye.net/opinion/where-palestines-martin-luther-king-shot-or-jailed-israel.

Agha, Ihsan Khalil. *Khan Yunis wa shuhada'iha* [*Khan Younis Martyrs*]. Cairo: Markaz Fajr Publishing, 1997.

Ahmed, Nasim. "Remembering the Sabra and Shatila Massacre." *Middle East Monitor*, September 16, 2019. https://www.middleeastmonitor.com/20190916-remembering-the-sabra-and-shatila-massacre/.

Albatta, Madeeha Hafez. *A White Lie*. Edited by Barbara Bill and Ghada Ageel. Edmonton: University of Alberta Press, 2020.

Allouche, Yasmina. "Remembering the 1952 Egyptian Revolution." *MEM*, July 23, 2017. https://www.middleeastmonitor.com/20170723-remembering-the-1952-egyptian-revolution/.

Alterman, Jon B. "Sadat and His Legacy: Egypt and the World, 1977–1997." *The Washington Institute for Near East Policy*, April 1, 1998. https://www.washingtoninstitute.org/policy-analysis/sadat-and-his-legacy-egypt-and-world-1977-1997.

Antonius, George. *The Arab Awakening: The Story of the Arab National Movement*. New York: Capricorn Books, 1965.

"The Assassination of Abu Jihad." *Journal of Palestine Studies* 17, no. 4 (Summer 1988): 146–47. doi:10.2307/2537305.

BADIL. *Survey of Palestinian Refugees and Internally Displaced Persons 2016–2018*. Vol. IX. Bethlehem: BADIL Resource Center for Palestinian Residency & Refugee Rights, 2019. http://www.

badil.org/phocadownloadpap/badil-new/publications/survay/
survey2016-2018-eng.pdf.

Barghouti, Mourid. *I Was Born There, I Was Born Here*. New York:
Walker & Company, 2012.

Baroud, Ramzy. "Gaza: Resistance through Poetry." *Counter Punch*,
June 17, 2016. https://www.counterpunch.org/2016/06/17/
gaza-resistance-through-poetry/.

———. "History from Below." PHD diss., Exeter University, 2015.

———. *My Father Was a Freedom Fighter: Gaza's Untold Story*.
London: Pluto Press, 2010.

———, ed. *Searching Jenin: Eyewitness Accounts of the Israeli Invasion*.
Seattle: Cune Press, 2003.

Barret, Roby. "Intervention in Iraq: 1958–1959." *Middle East
Institute*, April 1, 2008. https://mei.edu/publications/
intervention-iraq-1958-1959.

BBC News. "Abu Jihad Killing: Israeli Censor Releases Commando's
Account." BBC, November 1, 2012. https://www.bbc.com/news/
world-middle-east-20172511.

Bennet, James. "Arafat Not Present at Gaza Headquarters." *The New
York Times*, December 3, 2001. https://www.nytimes.
com/2001/12/03/international/arafat-not-present-at-gaza-
headquarters.html.

Benvenisti, Meron. *Sacred Landscape: The Buried History of the Holy
Land Since 1948*. Berkley: University of California Press, 2002.

"The Bombing of Beirut," *Journal of Palestine Studies* 11, no. 1 (1981):
218–25, doi:10.2307/2536065.

Bowen, Jeremy. "1967 War: Six Days that Changed the Middle East."
BBC, June 5, 2017. https://www.bbc.com/news/
world-middle-east-39960461.

Brown, Seyom. *Faces of Power: Constancy and Change in United
States Foreign Policy from Truman to Obama*, 3rd ed. New York:
Columbia University Press, 2015.

Bseiso, Mu'in. *88 Days Behind the Barricades (Thamaniya wa thamanoun yowman khalf al matarees)*. Beirut: Dar Al Farabi, 1985.

———. *Mu'in Bseiso: Entre l'épi et le fusil* [Between the Ear and the Gun]. Tunis: Lotus, 1988.

Bshara, Khaldun. "The Ottoman Saraya: All That Did Not Remain." *Jerusalem Quarterly* 69 (Spring 2017): 66–77. https://oldwebsite. palestine-studies.org/sites/default/files/jq-articles/Pages%20 from%20JQ%2069%20-%20Bshara.pdf.

Bshara, Khaldun and Shukri Arraf. *All That Did Not Remain*. Ramallah: Riwaq, 2016.

Btselem. "Israel Commits a Crime and Paints Palestinians as Lawbreakers: The Homes of 44 Palestinians, Including 22 Children, Were Demolished Yesterday in the West Bank." *Btselem*, November 26, 2020. https://www.btselem.org/ press_releases/20201126_44_palesinian_homes_demolished_ israel_commits_crime_and_paints_palestinians_as_the_ offenders.

———. "Summary." *Through No Fault of Their Own: Israel's Punitive House Demolitions in the al-Aqsa Intifada*. Jerusalem, Israel: Btselem, November 2004. https://www.btselem.org/ publications/summaries/200411_punitive_house_demolitions.

Burn, Rebecca. "Absent Memory: A Study of the Historiography of the Lebanese Civil War of 1975–1990." B.A. thesis, Wesleyan University, 2012. https://pdfs.semanticscholar.org/ fb16/4df7ff2daa157025e87906052133485f790f.pdf.

Chaitin, Julia. "Oral History." In *SAGE Encyclopedia of Qualitative Research Methods*, edited by Lisa M. Given. Thousand Oaks, CA: SAGE Publications, Inc., 2008. doi:10.4135/9781412963909. n301.

Cobban, Helena. "Roots of Resistance: The First Intifada in the Context of Palestinian History." *Mondoweiss*, December 17, 2012. https://mondoweiss.net/2012/12/roots-of-resistance-the-first-intifada-in-the-context-of-palestinian-history/.

Collins, Carole. "Chronology of the Israeli War in Lebanon September-December 1982." *Journal of Palestine Studies* 12, no. 2 (Winter 1983): 86–159. https://doi.org/10.2307/2536420.

"Cultural Heritage." *UNDP FOCUS* 1 (2004). https://fanack.com/wp-pdf-reader.php?pdf_src=/wp-content/uploads/2014/archive/user_upload/Documenten/Links/Occupied_Palestinian_Territories/UNDP_Focus_2004.pdf.

Damen, Rawan, Film dir. *Al-Nakba.* 2008; Qatar: Al Jazeera Arabic; 2013; reversioned by Al Jazeera World to English. Documentary film. https://interactive.aljazeera.com/aje/palestineremix/al-nakba.html#/17.

Darwish, Mahmoud. "Those Who Pass Between Fleeting Words." *Middle East Report* 154, September/October 1988. https://merip.org/1988/09/those-who-pass-between-fleeting-words/.

Dearden, Lizzie. "Israel-Gaza Conflict: University Hit as Palestinians Endure More Than 200 Strikes in 24 Hours." *Independent*, August 2, 2014. https://www.independent.co.uk/news/world/middle-east/israel-gaza-conflict-university-hit-as-palestinians-endure-more-than-200-strikes-in-24-hours-9644243.html.

Deeb II, Dennis J. *Israel, Palestine, and the Quest for Middle East Peace.* Maryland: University Press of America, 2013.

Dugard, John, and John Reynolds. "Apartheid, International Law, and the Occupied Palestinian Territory." *European Journal of International Law* 24, no. 3 (August 2013): 867–913. https://doi.org/10.1093/ejil/cht045.

Edelist, Ran, Film dir. *The Shaked Spirit.* 2007.

El-Haddad, Laila. *Gaza Mom: Palestine, Politics, Parenting, and Everything In Between.* Charlottesville, VA: Just World Books, 2010.

Fantappie, Maria, and Brittany Tanasa. "Oral Historian Rosemary Sayigh Records Palestine's Her-Story in *Voices: Palestinian Women Narrate Displacement.*" *Wowwire* (blog). *W4*, September

20, 2011. https://www.w4.org/en/wowwire/
palestinian-women-narrate-displacement-rosemary-sayigh/.

"The 55th Festival of Carthage Excites Tunisia." *Atlantico*, July 9,
2019. Accessed February 10, 2021. https://atlanticoonline.com/
en/the-55th-festival-of-carthage-excites-tunisia/.

Filiu, Jean-Pierre. *Gaza: A History*. Oxford: Oxford University Press,
2014.

———. *Pity the Nation: Lebanon at War*. Oxford: Oxford University
Press, 2001.

Gluck, Sherna Berger. "Oral History and al-Nakbah." The Oral
History Review 35, no. 1 (2008): 68–80.

Gramsci, Antonio. *Selections from the Prison Notebooks of Antonio
Gramsci*. New York: International Publishers, 1971.

Halbfinger, David M., Isabel Kershner, and Declan Walsh. "Israel
Kills Dozens at Gaza Border as U.S. Embassy Opens in
Jerusalem." *The New York Times*, May 14, 2018. https://www.
nytimes.com/2018/05/14/world/middleeast/gaza-protests-
palestinians-us-embassy.html.

Hassan, Othman. "Mu'in Bseiso: Quwwit al kalima taqhar jahim al
quyood" [Mu'in Bseiso: The power of the word conquers the hell
of chains]. *Alkhaleej*, May 15, 2018. https://www.alkhaleej.ae/
node/pdf/651253/pdf.

Hijazi, Ihsan A. "Israel Looted Archives of P.L.O., Officials Say." *The
New York Times*, October 1, 1982. https://www.nytimes.
com/1982/10/01/world/israeli-looted-archives-of-plo-
officials-say.html.

Helmy, Heba. "Streets of Cairo: Nahdet Misr Street, A Reflection of
Modern Egypt." *Egypt Independent*, November 5, 2011. https://
ww.egyptindependent.com/streets-cairo-nahdet-misr-street-
reflection-modern-egypt/.

Hilal, Jamil. "PLO Institutions: The Challenge Ahead." *Journal of
Palestine Studies* 23, no. 1 (Autumn 1993): 46–60.

Hroub, Khaled. *Hamas: Political Thought and Practice*. Washington,
DC: Institute for Palestine Studies, 2000.

Hughes, Matthew. *Britain's Pacification of Palestine: The British Army, the Colonial State, and the Arab Revolt, 1936–1939.* Military History Series. Cambridge: Cambridge University Press, 2019.

Humphries, Isabelle, and Laleh Khalili. "Gender of Nakba Memory." In *Nakba: Palestine, 1948, and the Claims of Memory*, edited by Ahmad H. Sa'di and Lila Abu-Lughod, 207–28. New York: Columbia University Press, 2007.

Hunt, Patrick. "Carthage, Ancient City, Tunisia." *Encyclopedia Britannica Online.* Accessed February 10, 2021. https://www.britannica.com/place/Carthage-ancient-city-Tunisia.

IMEU. "Discrimination Against Palestinian Citizens of Israel." *Institute for Middle East Understanding*, September 28, 2011. https://imeu.org/article/discrimination-against-palestinian-citizens-of-israel.

"Israeli Colonies and Israeli Colonial Expansion." CJPME Factsheet Series No. 9. *Canadians for Justice and Peace in the Middle East*, 2005. https://www.cjpme.org/fs_009.

"Israel Declines to Study Rabin Tie to Beatings." *The New York Times,* July 12, 1990. https://www.nytimes.com/1990/07/12/world/israel-declines-to-study-rabin-tie-to-beatings.html.

Jones, Peter M. "George Lefebvre and the Peasant Revolution: Fifty Years On." *French Historical Studies* 16, no. 3 (Spring, 1990): 645–63.

———. "'The Worst Spot in Gaza': 'You Will Not Understand How Hard it is Here' Until You See This Checkpoint." *Salon*, May 31, 2015. https://www.salon.com/2015/05/31/the_worst_spot_in_gaza_you_will_not_understand_how_hard_it_is_here_until_you_see_this_checkpoint/.

Kassem, Fatma. *Palestinian Women: Narrative Histories and Gender Memory.* London: Zed Books, 2011.

Kassim, Anis F., ed. *The Palestinian Yearbook of International Law, 1998–1999,* vol. 10. The Hague: Kluwer Law International, 2000.

Khalidi, Rashid. *The Iron Cage: The Story of the Palestinian Struggle for Statehood.* Boston: Beacon, 2006.

Khalidi, Walid, ed. *All That Remains: The Palestinian Villages Occupied and Depopulated by Israel in 1948*. Washington, DC: Institute for Palestine Studies, 1992.

———. *Before Their Diaspora: A Photographic History of the Palestinians, 1876–1948*. Washington, DC: Institute for Palestine Studies, 1984.

Khoury, Elias. "Remembering Ghassan Kanafani, or How a Nation Was Born of Story Telling." *Journal of Palestine Studies* 42, no. 3 (Spring 2013): 85–91.

Kifner, John. "Israel Detains 2 In Burial Alive of Palestinians." *The New York Times*, February 16, 1988. https://www.nytimes.com/1988/02/16/world/israel-detains-2-in-burial-alive-of-palestinians.html.

Kimmerling, Baruch. *Politicide: Ariel Sharon's War Against the Palestinians*. London: Verso, 2003.

LeBlanc, John Randolph. *Edward Said on the Prospects of Peace in Palestine and Israel*. New York: Palgrave MacMilllan, 2013.

LeVine, Mark. "Tracing Gaza's Chaos to 1948." *Al Jazeera*, July 13, 2009. https://www.aljazeera.com/focus/arabnity/2008/02/2008525185737842919.html.

Lightman, Alan. "The Role of the Public Intellectual." *MIT Communications Forum*. Accessed February 11, 2021. http://web.mit.edu/comm-forum/legacy/papers/lightman.html.

Luft, Gal. "The Logic of Israel's Targeted Killing." *Middle East Quarterly* 10, no.1 (Winter 2003): 3–13. http://www.meforum.org/article/515.

Macintyre, Donald. "By 2020, the UN Said Gaza Would be Unliveable. Did It Turn Out that Way?" *The Guardian*, December 28, 2019. https://www.theguardian.com/world/2019/dec/28/gaza-strip-202-unliveable-un-report-did-it-turn-out-that-way.

Masalha, Nur. *The Palestine Nakba: Decolonising History, Narrating the Subaltern, Reclaiming Memory*. London and New York: Zed Books, 2012.

Morris, Benny. *Israel's Border Wars, 1949-1956*. Oxford: Clarendon Press, 1993.

Muhajrani, Ataallah. "Ila Al Mutamawit—Samih Al Qasim" [To the dead—Samih Al Qasim]. *Alsharq Alawsat*, August 25, 2014. https://aawsat.com/home/article/167221.

Murray, Eóin. "Under Siege." In *Defending Hope: Dispatches from the Front Lines in Palestine and Israel*, edited by Eóin Murray and James Mehigan, 29-46. Dublin: Veritas Books, 2018.

"Nakba's Oral History Interviews Listing." *Palestine Remembered*, March 31, 2004. https://www.palestineremembered.com/ OralHistory/Interviews-Listing/Story1151.html.

Nimr, Sonia. "Fast Forward to the Past: A Look into Palestinian Collective Memory." *Cahiers de Littérature Orale* 63-64 (January 2008): 338-49. https://doi.org/10.4000/clo.287.

"Oral History: Defined." *Oral History Association*. Accessed February 11, 2021. https://www.oralhistory.org/about/ do-oral-history/.

Osman, Tarek. *Egypt on the Brink*. New Haven and London: Yale University Press, 2010.

Pappe, Ilan. *The Ethnic Cleansing of Palestine*. Oxford: One World Publications, 2006.

"Political Economy of Palestine." *Institute for Palestine Studies*. Accessed February 11, 2021. https://oldwebsite.palestine-studies. org/ar/node/198424.

Randal, Jonathan, C. "Assassination of PLO Aide Raises Many Questions." *Washington Post,* July 10, 1992. https://www. washingtonpost.com/archive/politics/1992/07/10/ assassination-of-plo-aide-raises-many-questions/ c482bb3e-a437-474d-9835-421397ce87bf/?noredirect=on&utm_ term=.8785a980fce8.

Roy, Sara. "The Gaza Strip: A Case of Economic De-Development." *Journal of Palestine Studies* 17, no. 1 (Autumn 1987): 56-88.

Sa'di, Ahmad H., and Lila Abu-Lughod. "Introduction: The Claims of Memory." In *Nakba: Palestine, 1948, and the Claims of*

Memory, edited by Ahmad H. Sa'di and Lila Abu-Lughod, 1–24. New York: Columbia University Press, 2007.

———. *Nakba: Palestine, 1948, and the Claims of Memory*. New York: Columbia University Press, 2007.

Said, Edward W. "Invention, Memory and Place." *Critical Inquiry* 26, no. 2 (Winter 2000): 175–92.

———. *Covering Islam: How the Media and the Experts Determine How We See the Rest of the World*. New York: Pantheon Books, 1981.

———. "On Palestinian Identity: A Conversation with Salman Rushdie (1986)." In *The Politics of Dispossession: The Struggle for Palestinian Self Determination, 1969–1994*, 107–29. New York: Pantheon Books, 1994.

———. "Permission to Narrate." *Journal of Palestine Studies* 13, no. 3 (Spring 1984): 27–48.

Sayigh, Rosemary. "Oral History, Colonialist Dispossession, and the State: the Palestinian Case." *Settler Colonial Studies* 5, no. 3 (2015): 193–204.

———. *The Palestinians: From Peasants to Revolutionaries*. London: Zed Books, 1979.

———. *Voices: Palestinian Women Narrate Displacement*. Al-Mashriq, 2005/2007. https://almashriq.hiof.no/palestine/300/301/voices/.

Seelye, Talcott W. "Special Report: Ben Ali Visit Marks Third Stage in 200-Year-Old US-Tunisian Special Relationship." *Washington Report on Middle East Affairs*, March 1990. https://www.wrmea.org/1990-march/ben-ali-visit-marks-third-stage-in-200-year-old-us-tunisian-special-relationship.html.

Shabi, Rachel. "Understanding Israel through its Marginalised Mizrahi Jews." *TRT World*, June 28, 2017. https://www.trtworld.com/opinion/understanding-israel-through-the-marginalised-mizrahi-jews-389035.

Shlaim, Avi. "How Israel Brought Gaza to the Brink of Humanitarian Catastrophe." *The Guardian*, January 7, 2009. https://www.

theguardian.com/world/2009/jan/07/gaza-israel-palestine. Also
published as "Background and Context." *Journal of Palestine
Studies* 38, no. 3 (Spring 2009): 223–39. doi:10.1525/jps.2009.
xxxviii.3.223.

Shwaikh, Malaka Mohammad. "Gaza Remembers: Narratives of
Displacement in Gaza's Oral History." In *An Oral History of the
Palestinian Nakba*, edited by Nahla Abdo and Nur Masalha,
277–93. London: Zed Books, 2018. https://www.researchgate.
net/publication/329130803_Narratives_of_Displacement_
in_Gaza's_Oral_History_2.

Sluglett, Marion Farouk, and Peter Sluglett. *Iraq Since 1958: From
Revolution to Dictatorship*. New York: IB Tauris, 1990.

"The State of the World's Refugees 2006: Human Displacement in
the New Millennium." *United Nations High Commissioner for
Refugees*, April 20, 2006. https://www.unhcr.org/publications/
sowr/4a4dc1a89/state-worlds-refugees-2006-human-
displacement-new-millennium.html.

Steele, Jonathan. "The Tragedy of Jenin." *The Guardian*, August 2,
2002. https://www.theguardian.com/world/2002/aug/02/
israel2.

"Study Says Attacks on Infrastructure in Gaza and West Bank Exact
a Human Cost." Nicholas School of the Environment, Duke
University, February 18, 2019. https://nicholas.duke.edu/news/
study-says-attacks-infrastructure-gaza-and-west-bank-exact-
human-cost.

Tahhan, Zena. "The *Naksa*: How Israel Occupied the Whole of
Palestine in 1967." *Al Jazeera*, June 4, 2018. https://www.
aljazeera.com/indepth/features/2017/06/50-years-israeli-
occupation-longest-modern-history-170604111317533.html.

Tempest, Rone. "PLO Official Assassinated on Paris Street." Los
Angeles Times, June 9, 1992. https://www.latimes.com/archives/
la-xpm-1992-06-09-mn-182-story.html.

"32 Years Since Israel Bombed Hammam Chott." *MEM*, October 2,
2017. https://www.middleeastmonitor.com/20171002-32-years-
since-the-zionist-bombing-of-hammam-chott/.

Thomson, Alistair. "Four Paradigm Transformations in Oral
History." *The Oral History Review* 34, no. 1 (2007): 49-70.

Thompson, Paul. *The Voice of the Past: Oral History.* Oxford: Oxford
University Press, 1978.

"Timeline: The Humanitarian Impact of the Gaza Blockade." *Oxfam
International.* Accessed February 11, 2021. https://www.oxfam.
org/en/timeline-humanitarian-impact-gaza-blockade.

Tran, Mark. "Israel Declares Gaza 'Enemy Entity.'" *The Guardian*,
September 19, 2007. https://www.theguardian.com/
world/2007/sep/19/usa.israel1.

Trew, Bel. "The UN Said Gaza Would be Uninhabitable by 2020—In
Truth, It Already Is." *Independent*, December 29, 2019. https://
www.independent.co.uk/voices/israel-palestine-gaza-hamas-
protests-hospitals-who-un-a9263406.html.

United Nations. "Summary." *Middle East—UNEF 1: Background.*
https://peacekeeping.un.org/en/mission/past/unef1backgr1.
html.

United Nations. *Gaza in 2020: A Liveable Place?* August 2012.
https://www.unrwa.org/userfiles/file/publications/gaza/
Gaza%20in%202020.pdf.

UN General Assembly. *Resolution 194 (III): Palestine—Progress
Report of the United Nations Mediator.* December 11, 1948.
https://unispal.un.org/dpa/dpr/unispal.nsf/0/
c758572b78d1cd0085256bcf0077e51a.

Veeser, H. Aram. *Edward Said: The Charisma of Criticism.* London:
Routledge, 2010.

Weill, Sharon. "The Targeted Killing of Salah Shehadeh: From Gaza
to Madrid." *Journal of International Criminal Justice* 7, no. 3
(2009): 617-31.

Weizman, Eyal. "The Architecture of Ariel Sharon: Sharon Leaves
Behind a Legacy of Construction and Destruction That Has

Shaped Today's Israel and Palestine." *Al-Jazeera*, January 11,
2014. https://www.aljazeera.com/indepth/opinion/2014/01/
architecture-ariel-sharon-2014111141710308855.html.

"Where We Work, Gaza Strip." *United Nations Relief and Works
Agency for Palestine Refugees in the Near East*. Accessed February
11, 2021. https://www.unrwa.org/where-we-work/gaza-strip.

Woodward, Bob. "Alliance with a Lebanese Leader." *Washington
Post,* September 29, 1987. https://www.washingtonpost.com/
archive/politics/1987/09/29/alliance-with-a-lebanese-leader/
ab94dec7-2029-409b-8ebd-cbf954318cc1/?utm_
term=.0ce6f06d9a13.

"World Bank Warns, Gaza Economy is 'Collapsing.'" *Al Jazeera*,
September 25, 2016. https://www.aljazeera.com/news/2018/09/
world-bank-warns-gaza-economy-collapsing-180925085246106.
html.

Zogby, James. "The Sins and Horrors of 1967 Are Alive Today." *The
National*, June 17, 2017. https://www.thenational.ae/opinion/
the-sins-and-horrors-of-1967-are-alive-today-1.50209.

Other Titles from University of Alberta Press

A White Lie

MADEEHA HAFEZ ALBATTA

Edited by Barbara Bill & Ghada Ageel

The personal story of a brave Palestinian woman's fight for dignity and freedom.

Women's Voices from Gaza Series

Apartheid in Palestine

Hard Laws and Harder Experiences

Edited by GHADA AGEEL

Palestinian, Israeli, academic, and activist voices gather to humanize ongoing debates over Israel and Palestine.

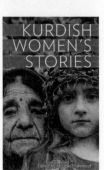

Kurdish Women's Stories

Edited by HOUZAN MAHMOUD

From all four parts of Kurdistan and across the diaspora, Kurdish women tell their stories.

More information at uap.ualberta.ca